BBC ACTIVE

GET BY in GREEK

ANTIGONE VELTSIDOU BENTHAM
CLIVE ALDISS with
YOULA NOTIA and MATTHEW HANCOCK
LANGUAGE CONSULTANT
SOPHIA ECONOMIDES

Published by BBC Active, an imprint of Educational Publishers LLP, part of the Pearson Education Group, Edinburgh Gate, Harlow, Essex CM20 2JE, England

First edition published 1998. This edition published 2007. Reprinted 2007, 2008.

ISBN: 978-1-4066-1266-0

Cover design: Emma Wallace
Cover photograph: FAN Travelstock/Alamy
Insides concept design: Nicolle Thomas
Layout: Jo Digby, Rob Lian
Commissioning editor: Debbie Marshall
Project editor: Melanie Kramers
Project assistant: Hannah Beatson
Editor: Penny Papadopoulou
Senior production controller: Man Fai Lau
Marketing: Fiona Griffiths, Paul East
Audio producer for the new edition: Martin Williamson, Prolingua Productions
Sound engineer: Dave Morritt, at Studio AVP
Presenters: Maria Dikeakou-Gaffeny, Tassos Spiridakis, Vanda Rapti, Manolis Emmanouel, DeNica Fairman, Bill Dufris, Jane Whittenshaw
Original audio producer: John Green, tefl tapes
Original sound engineer and music: Tim Woolf
Printed and bound in China (CTPSC/06).
The Publisher's policy is to use paper manufactured from sustainable forests.

All photographs supplied by Alamy Images.
p8 David Crausby; p10 IML Image Group Ltd; p13 Jon Arnold Images; p15 isifa Image Service s.r.o.; p19 mediacolor's; p24 Rob Rayworth; p27 IML Image Group Ltd; p30 Elmtree Images; p32 Andre Jenny; p34 George Blonsky; p40 colinspics; p44 Robert Harding Picture Library Ltd; p47 FAN travelstock; p49 Moritz Steiger; p50 Nic Cleave Photography; p54 Terry Harris just Greece photo library; p56 Wilmar Photography; p58 Huw Jones; p60 Kalpana Kartik; p64 Pixida; p71 PCL; p72 Terry Harris just Greece photo library; p74 Profimedia International s.r.o.; p81 Peter Adams Photography; p83 GreekFoodStock; p85 Terry Harris just Greece photo library; p87 Ian Dagnall; p89 Robert Harding Picture Library Ltd; p96 foodfolio; p101 IML Image Group Ltd; p103 Stock Connection Distribution; p105 Peter Horree; p108 Sean Burke; p110 FAN travelstock; p112 FAN travelstock; p117 vario images GmbH & Co.KG; p125 Aflo Foto Agency; p127 Bruce yuanyue Bi.

Contents

How to **use this book**

Get By in Greek is divided into colour-coded topics to help you find what you need quickly. Each unit contains practical travel tips to help you get around and understand the country, and a **phrasemaker**, to help you say what you need to and understand what you hear.

As well as listing key phrases, **Get By in Greek** aims to help you understand how the language works so that you can build your own phrases and start to communicate independently. The **check out** dialogues within each section show the language in action, and the **try it out** activities give you an opportunity to practise for yourself. The **link up** sections pick out the key structures and give helpful notes about their use. A round-up of all the basic grammar can be found in the **Language Builder**, pp132-139.

In Greek, all nouns – things, people, concepts – are either masculine, feminine or neuter, and this affects other words related to them, such as the words for 'the' and 'a'. There are also often masculine and feminine versions of people's occupations and nationalities, shown in this book as, for example: **Άγγλος/Αγγλίδα**, meaning English man/English woman.

If you've bought the pack with the audio CD, you'll be able to listen to a selection of the most important phrases and **check out** dialogues, as well as all the **as if you were there** activities. You can use the book on its own, but the CD will help you to improve your pronunciation.

sounds Greek

The good thing about Greek pronunciation is that the written form and the spoken form of the language are very similar. Each letter is usually pronounced in the same way each time you see it. This book uses a pronunciation guide, based on sounds you already know, to help you start speaking Greek. Key points to remember are also highlighted in the **sound checks** throughout the units.

stress

Stressing the right parts of words in Greek helps people to understand more easily what you are saying. Accents in written Greek show where the stress falls. In this book the stressed syllable is shown in bold type:

βούτυρο *v**oo**teero*   **Αθήνα** *ath**ee**na*   **παρακαλώ** *parakal**o***

... Greek alphabet consists of 24 letters, most of which have approximate ...valent sounds in English. These are shown here in upper and lower case.

vowels

	sounds like ...	shown as ...
Α α	'a' in 'man'	*a*
Ε ε	'e' in 'pen'	*e*
Η η	'ee' in 'meet' (clipped short)	*ee*
Ι ι	'ee' in 'meet' (clipped short)	*ee*
Ο ο	'o' in 'hot'	*o*
Υ υ	'ee' in 'meet' (clipped short)	*ee*
Ω ω	'o' in 'hot'	*o*

Note that some letters or combinations of letters have the same sound:

- **αι** and **ε** both sound like 'e' in 'pen'.
- **ο** and **ω** both sound like 'o' in 'hot'.
- **ι**, **η**, **υ**, **ει** and **οι** all sound like 'ee' in 'meet' clipped short.

consonants

	sounds like ...	shown as ...
Β β	'v' in 'van'	*v*
Γ γ	'wh' in 'what' or	*gh*
	'y' in yes before the sounds 'e' and 'ee'	*y*
Δ δ	'th' in 'that'	*dh*
Ζ ζ	'z' in 'zoo'	*z*
Θ θ	'th' in 'thin'	*th*
Κ κ	'k' in 'kit'	*k*
Λ λ	'l' in 'line'	*l*
Μ μ	'm' in 'mat'	*m*
Ν ν	'n' in 'not'	*n*
Ξ ξ	'x' in 'box'	*ks*
Π π	'p' in 'pin'	*p*
Ρ ρ	'r' in 'rum'	*r*
Σ σ (ς*)	's' in 'set' or	*s*
	'z' in 'zoo' before **β**, **γ**, **δ**, **ζ**, **μ**, **ν**, **ρ** in the middle of a word	*z*
Τ τ	't' in 'top'	*t*
Φ φ	'f' in 'fat'	*f*
Χ χ	'ch' in 'loch'	*h*
Ψ ψ	'ps' in 'perhaps'	*ps*

* When **σ** occurs at the end of words, it is replaced by **ς**.

combinations of letters

	sounds like ...	shown as ...
αι	'e' in 'pen '	*e*
ει, οι	'ee' in 'meet' (clipped short)	*ee*
αυ	'af' in 'after' before **θ**, **κ**, **ξ**, **π**, **σ**, **τ**, **φ**, **χ**, **ψ**	*af*
	or 'av' in average before **θ**, **κ**, **ξ**, **π**, **σ**, **τ**, **φ**, **χ**, **ψ** or a vowel	*av*
ευ	like 'ef' in 'theft' before **θ**, **κ**, **ξ**, **π**, **σ**, **τ**, **φ**, **χ**, **ψ**	*ef*
	or 'ev' in 'every' before **θ**, **κ**, **ξ**, **π**, **σ**, **τ**, **φ**, **χ**, **ψ** or a vowel	*ev*
ου	'oo' in shoot	*oo*
γγ	'ng' in England	*ng*
γκ	'ng' in 'England' in the middle of a word	*ng*
	or 'g' in 'get' after a consonant, or at the start of a word	*g*
γχ	'nh' in 'inherent'	*nh*
μπ	'mb' in 'slumber' in the middle of a word	*mb*
	or 'b' in 'bed' at the start of a word	*b*
ντ	'nd' in 'bending' in the middle of a word or 'd' in door at the start	*nd* *d*
τς	'ts' in 'cats'	*ts*
τζ	'ds' in 'seeds'	*ds*

alphabet

Here's a guide to pronouncing the Greek alphabet.

Α *alfa*	**Β** *veeta*	**Γ** *ghama*	**Δ** *dhelta*	**Ε** *epseelon*	**Ζ** *zeeta*
Η *eeta*	**Θ** *theeta*	**Ι** *yeeota*	**Κ** *kapa*	**Λ** *lamdha*	**Μ** *mee*
Ν *nee*	**Ξ** *ksee*	**Ο** *omeekron*	**Π** *pee*	**Ρ** *ro*	**Σ** *seeghma*
Τ *taf*	**Υ** *eepseelon*	**Φ** *fee*	**Χ** *hee*	**Ψ** *psee*	**Ω** *omegha*

Bare **Necessities**

phrasemaker

greetings

you may say …

Good morning!	Καλημέρα!	*kaleemera*
Good evening!	Καλησπέρα!	*kaleespera*
Good night!	Καληνύχτα!	*kaleeneehta*
Hello! or Goodbye! (informal/formal)	Γεια σου! (sing)/ Γεια σας! (pl)	*ya soo/ ya sas*
How are you? (informal/formal)	Τι κάνεις; (sing)/ Τι κάνετε; (pl)	*tee kanees/ tee kanete*
Very well, thank you.	Πολύ καλά, ευχαριστώ.	*polee kala efhareesto*

other useful words

you may say …

yes/no	ναι/όχι	*ne/ohee*
please	παρακαλώ	*parakalo*
thanks (very much)	ευχαριστώ (πολύ)	*efhareesto (polee)*
certainly	μάλιστα	*maleesta*
You're welcome.	Παρακαλώ.	*parakalo*
excuse me/sorry	συγνώμη	*seeghnomee*
of course	βεβαίως	*veveos*
okay	εντάξει	*endaksee*
Here (you are/it is).	Ορίστε.	*oreeste*
It's all right/It doesn't matter.	Δεν πειράζει.	*dhen peerazee*
Don't mention it.	Παρακαλώ.	*parakalo*

where is/are ...?

you may say ...

Where is ...	Πού είναι ...	*poo **ee**ne*
the museum?	το μουσείο;	*to moos**ee**o*
the nearest bank?	η πιο κοντινή τράπεζα;	*ee pee**o** kondeen**ee** tr**a**peza*
Is there ...	Υπάρχει ...	*eep**a**rhee*
a telephone?	τηλέφωνο;	*teel**e**fono*
a shower?	ντους;	*doos*
Are there ...	Υπάρχουν ...	*eep**a**rhoon*
any toilets?	τουαλέτες;	*tooal**e**tes*

you may hear ...

Είναι ...	***ee**ne*	It's ...
ίσια.	***ee**seea*	straight on.
δεξιά.	*dhekseea**a***	on the right.
αριστερά.	*areester**a***	on the left.
Πού θέλετε να πάτε;	*poo th**e**lete na p**a**te*	Where would you like to go?
Συγνώμη, δεν ξέρω.	*seeghn**o**mee dhen ks**e**ro*	I'm sorry, I don't know.

check out 1

You ask a passer-by for directions to the bank.

- ❍ Συγνώμη, πού είναι η πιο κοντινή τράπεζα;
  seeghnomee poo eene ee peeo kondeenee trapeza
- \- Είναι αριστερά.
  eene areestera
- ❍ Ευχαριστώ πολύ.
  efhareesto polee
- \- Παρακαλώ.
  parakalo

Q Where is the bank?

do you have ...?

you may say ...

Do you have ... any oranges? any postcards?	Έχετε ... πορτοκάλια; κάρτες;	*ehete portokaleea kartes*
Do you have ... a map? a double room?	Έχετε ... χάρτη; δίκλινο δωμάτιο;	*ehete hartee dheekleeno dhomateeo*

I'd like ...

you may say ...

I'd like ... a ticket to Thessaloniki.	Θέλω ... ένα εισιτήριο για τη Θεσσαλονίκη.	*thelo ena eeseeteereeo ya tee thesaloneekee*
I'd like ... a kilo of apples. two kilos of apples.	Μου δίνετε ... ένα κιλό μήλα. δύο κιλά μήλα.	*moo dheenete ena keelo meela dheeo keela meela*
I'd like this one/ that one.	Θέλω αυτό/εκείνο.	*thelo afto/ekeeno*

how much?

you may say ...

How much is it/that?	Πόσο κάνει αυτό;	p**o**so k**a**nee aft**o**
How much are they/ these?	Πόσο κάνουν αυτά;	p**o**so k**a**noon aft**a**

getting things straight

you may say ...

Pardon?	Ορίστε;/ Συγνώμη;	or**ee**ste/ seeghn**o**mee
Could you say that again, please?	Το επαναλαμβάνετε, παρακαλώ;	to epanalamv**a**nete parakal**o**
More slowly, please.	Πιο αργά, παρακαλώ.	pee**o** argh**a** parakal**o**
I don't understand.	Δεν καταλαβαίνω.	dhen katalav**e**no
I speak a little Greek.	Μιλάω λίγα Ελληνικά.	meel**a**o l**ee**gha eleeneek**a**
Do you speak English?	Μιλάτε Αγγλικά;	meel**a**te angleek**a**
I don't know.	Δεν ξέρω.	dhen ks**e**ro

check out 2

You need to buy some groceries at the market.

- ❍ Καλημέρα.
  *kaleem**e**ra*
- \- Καλημέρα. Έχετε πορτοκάλια;
  *kaleem**e**ra. **e**hete portok**a**leea*
- ❍ Μάλιστα.
  *m**a**leesta*
- \- Μου δίνετε δύο κιλά;
  *moo dh**ee**nete dh**ee**o keel**a***
- ❍ Ορίστε.
  *or**ee**ste*
- \- Πόσο κάνουν;
  *p**o**so k**a**noon*
- ❍ Έξι ευρώ.
  e**ksee evr**o
- \- Ευχαριστώ. Γεια σας.
  *efhareest**o**. ya sas*
- ❍ Γεια σας.
  ya sas

Q What do you ask for?

talking about yourself

you may say ...

My name is ...	Λέγομαι ...	*l**e**ghome*
This is ...	Αυτός είναι ...	*aft**o**s **ee**ne*
my husband.	ο άντρας μου.	*o **a**ndras moo*
my son.	ο γιος μου.	*o yos moo*
This is ...	Αυτή είναι ...	*aft**ee** **ee**ne*
my wife.	η γυναίκα μου.	*ee gheen**e**ka moo*
my daughter.	η κόρη μου.	*ee k**o**ree moo*

Pleased to meet you.	Χαίρω πολύ.	h**e**ro pol**ee**
I'm from ... Wales.	Είμαι από ... την Ουαλία.	**ee**me ap**o** teen ooal**ee**a
I'm ... English. (See nationalities, p18)	Είμαι ... Άγγλος/Αγγλίδα.	**ee**me **a**nglos/angl**ee**dha
I'm on ... holiday. a business trip.	Είμαι σε ... διακοπές. επαγγελματικό ταξίδι.	**ee**me se dheeakop**e**s epangelmateek**o** taks**ee**dhee
I have ... children. two	Έχω ... παιδιά. δύο	**e**ho ... pedhee**a** dh**ee**o
I don't have children.	Δεν έχω παιδιά.	dhen **e**ho pedhee**a**
I am ... years old. (See numbers, p17)	Είμαι ... χρονών.	**ee**me ... hron**o**n
I am ... single. married. separated. divorced.	Είμαι ... ελεύθερος/ελεύθερη. παντρεμένος/παντρεμένη. χωρισμένος/χωρισμένη. διαζευγμένος/διαζευγμένη.	**ee**me el**e**ftheros/el**e**ftheree pandrem**e**nos/pandrem**e**nee horeezm**e**nos/horeezm**e**nee dheeazevghm**e**nos/dheeazevghm**e**nee
I have ... a boyfriend/girlfriend. a partner.	Έχω ... φίλο/φίλη. σύντροφο.	**e**ho f**ee**lo/f**ee**lee s**ee**ndrofo
I'm ... a nurse. a doctor. a student.	Είμαι ... νοσοκόμος/νοσοκόμα. γιατρός. φοιτητής/φοιτήτρια.	**ee**me nosok**o**mos/nosok**o**ma yatr**o**s feeteet**ee**s/feet**ee**treea
I work in ... a bank. a supermarket.	Δουλεύω σε ... τράπεζα. σουπερμάρκετ.	dhool**e**vo se tr**a**peza sooperm**a**rket

you may hear ...

Πώς σας λένε;	*pos sas **le**ne*	What's your name? (formal)
Πώς σε λένε;	*pos se **le**ne*	(informal)
Από πού;	*ap**o** poo*	Where from?
Από πού είσαστε;	*ap**o** poo **ee**saste*	Where are you from?
Τι δουλειά κάνετε;	*tee dhoolee**a** k**a**nete*	What do you do for a living?
Έχετε παιδιά;	***e**hete pedhee**a***	Do you have any children?
Είστε παντρεμένος/ παντρεμένη;	***ee**ste pandrem**e**nos/ pandrem**e**nee*	Are you married?
Πόσο χρονών είστε;	*p**o**so hron**o**n **ee**ste*	How old are you?
Είστε σε διακοπές;	***ee**ste se dheeakop**e**s*	Are you on holiday?
Σας αρέσει η Ελλάδα;	*sas ar**e**see ee el**a**dha*	Do you like Greece?

check out 3

You're staying in a hotel in Athens, and get chatting to another guest.

❍ Πώς σας λένε;
*pos sas **le**ne*

\- John Smith. Είμαι Άγγλος.
*john smith. **ee**me **a**nglos*

❍ Από πού;
*ap**o** poo*

\- Είμαι από το Manchester.
***ee**me ap**o** to Manchester*

❍ Είστε σε διακοπές ή σε επαγγελματικό ταξίδι;
***ee**ste se dheeakop**e**s ee se epangelmateek**o** taks**ee**dee*

\- Είμαι σε επαγγελματικό ταξίδι.
***ee**me se epangelmateek**o** taks**ee**dee*

❍ Τι δουλειά κάνετε;
*tee dhoolee**a** k**a**nete*

\- Δουλεύω σε τράπεζα.
*dhool**e**vo se tr**a**peza*

❍ Είστε παντρεμένος;
***ee**ste pandrem**e**nos*

\- Ναι. Έχω δύο παιδιά.
*ne. **e**ho dh**ee**o pedhee**a***

Q Are you in Greece on holiday or business?
How many children do you have?

changing money

you may say ...

What's the exchange rate for the pound?	Πόσο έχει η λίρα;	*p**o**so **e**hee ee l**ee**ra*
What's the commission charge?	Πόση προμήθεια χρεώνετε;	*p**o**see prom**ee**theea hre**o**nete*

I'd like to ...	Θέλω να αλλάξω ...	*thelo na alakso*
change £100.	εκατό λίρες.	*ekato leeres*
exchange some traveller's cheques.	ταξιδιωτικές επιταγές.	*takseedheeoteekes epeetaghes*

you may hear ...

Είναι ... ευρώ στη λίρα.	*eene ... evro stee leera*	It's at ... euros to the pound.
Χρεώνουμε 2% προμήθεια.	*hreonoome dheeo tees ekato promeetheea*	Commission is 2%.
Το διαβατήριό σας, παρακαλώ.	*to dheeavateereeo sas parakalo*	Your passport, please.

check out 4

You are changing some money at the bank.

- ❍ Πόσο έχει η λίρα;
  poso ehee ee leera
- \- Ένα ευρώ και σαράντα πέντε λεπτά.
  ena evro ke saranda pende lepta
- ❍ Θέλω να αλλάξω εκατό λίρες.
  thelo na alakso ekato leeres
- \- Εντάξει. Το διαβατήριό σας, παρακαλώ.
  endaksee. to dheeavateereeo sas parakalo

Q How much is £100 in euros?
What does the assistant ask for?

the time

you may say ...

When?	Πότε;	*pote*
What time is it?	Τι ώρα είναι;	*tee ora eene*
What time does it leave/arrive?	Τι ώρα φεύγει/φτάνει;	*tee ora fevyee/ftanee*

you may hear ...

Είναι ... μεσημέρι. μεσάνυχτα.	*eene meseemeree mesaneehta*	It's ... midday. midnight.
στη μία η ώρα	*stee meea ee ora*	at one o'clock
μία και δέκα	*meea ke dheka*	ten past one
δύο και τέταρτο	*deeo ke tetarto*	quarter past two
τρεις και μισή	*trees ke meesee*	half past three
τέσσερεις παρά τέταρτο	*teserees para tetarto*	quarter to four
το πρωί/βράδυ	*to proee/vradhee*	in the morning/ evening
σήμερα το μεσημέρι	*seemera to meseemeree*	this afternoon
αύριο	*avreeo*	tomorrow

months

January	Ιανουάριος	*eeanooareeos*
February	Φεβρουάριος	*fevrooareeos*
March	Μάρτιος	*marteeos*
April	Απρίλιος	*apreeleeos*
May	Μάιος	*maeeos*
June	Ιούνιος	*eeooneeos*
July	Ιούλιος	*eeooleeos*
August	Αύγουστος	*avgoostos*
September	Σεπτέμβριος	*septemvreeos*
October	Οκτώβριος	*oktovreeos*
November	Νοέμβριος	*noemvreeos*
December	Δεκέμβριος	*dhekemvreeos*

Bare **Necessities**

days of the week

Monday	Δευτέρα	*dheft**e**ra*
Tuesday	Τρίτη	*tr**ee**tee*
Wednesday	Τετάρτη	*tet**a**rtee*
Thursday	Πέμπτη	*p**e**mptee*
Friday	Παρασκευή	*paraskev**ee***
Saturday	Σάββατο	*s**a**vato*
Sunday	Κυριακή	*keereeak**ee***

numbers

1	ένας/μία (μια)/ένα	***e**nas/m**ee**a (mee**a**)/**e**na*
2	δύο (δυο)	*dh**ee**o (dh**ee**o)*
3	τρεις/τρεις/ τρία	*trees/trees/ tr**ee**a*
4	τέσσερεις/ τέσσερεις/ τέσσερα	*t**e**serees/ t**e**serees/ t**e**sera*
5	πέντε	*p**e**nde*
6	έξι	***e**ksee*
7	εφτά	*eft**a***
8	οχτώ	*oht**o***
9	εννέα	*en**e**a*
10	δέκα	*dh**e**ka*
11	έντεκα	***e**ndeka*
12	δώδεκα	*dh**o**dheka*
13	δεκατρείς/ δεκατρία	*dhekatr**ee**s/ dhekatr**ee**a*
14	δεκατέσσερεις/ δεκατέσσερα	*dhekat**e**serees /dhekat**e**sera*
15	δεκαπέντε	*dhekap**e**nde*
16	δεκαέξι	*dheka**e**ksee*
20	είκοσι	***ee**kosee*
21	εικοσιένα	*eekosee**e**na*
30	τριάντα	*tree**a**nda*
40	σαράντα	*sar**a**nda*
50	πενήντα	*pen**ee**nda*
60	εξήντα	*eks**ee**nda*
70	εβδομήντα	*evdhom**ee**nda*
80	ογδόντα	*ogdh**o**nda*
90	ενενήντα	*enen**ee**nda*
95	ενενήντα πέντε	*enen**ee**nda p**e**nde*

100	εκατό	*ekat**o***
200	διακόσια	*dheeak**o**seea*
208	διακόσια οχτώ	*dheeak**o**seea oht**o***
300	τριακόσια	*treeak**o**seea*
400	τετρακόσια	*tetrak**o**seea*
500	πεντακόσια	*pendak**o**seea*
600	εξακόσια	*eksak**o**seea*
700	εφτακόσια	*eftak**o**seea*
800	οχτακόσια	*ohtak**o**seea*
900	εννιακόσια	*enniak**o**seea*
1000	χίλια	*h**ee**leea*

(The numbers 2, 3, 4, 200, 300, 400, etc. change ending according to what they are referring to. Where three forms are given, these are masculine, feminine and neuter. For more details, see the Language Builder, p132.)

ordinal numbers

1st	πρώτος πρώτη πρώτο	*protos* *protee* *proto*
2nd	δεύτερος	*dhefteros*
3rd	τρίτος	*treetos*
4th	τέταρτος	*tetartos*
5th	πέμπτος	*pemptos*
6th	έκτος	*ektos*
7th	έβδομος	*evdhomos*
8th	όγδοος	*ogdhoos*
9th	ένατος	*enatos*
10th	δέκατος	*dhekatos*

countries & nationalities

Australia: Australian	Αυστραλία: Αυστραλός/ Αυστραλέζα	*afstraleea: afstralos/ afstraleza*
Canada: Canadian	Καναδάς: Καναδός/ Καναδέζα	*kanadhas: kanadhos/ kanadheza*
England: English	Αγγλία: Άγγλος/ Αγγλίδα	*angleea: anglos/ angleedha*
Great Britain: British	Μεγάλη Βρετανία: Βρετανός/Βρετανίδα	*megalee vretaneea: vretanos/vretaneedha*
Greece: Greek	Ελλάδα: Έλληνας/ Ελληνίδα	*eladha: eleenas/ eleeneedha*
New Zealand: New Zealander	Νέα Ζηλανδία: Νεοζηλανδός/ Νεοζηλανδή	*nea zeelandheea: neozeelandhos/ neozeelandhee*
(Northern) Ireland: Irish	(Βόρεια) Ιρλανδία: (Βορειο-) Ιρλανδός/ Ιρλανδή	*(voreea) eerlandheea: (voreeo) eerlandhos/ eerlandhee*
Scotland: Scottish	Σκωτία: Σκωτσέζος/ Σκωτσέζα	*skoteea: skotsezos/ skotseza*
South Africa: South African	Νότια Αφρική: Νοτιοαφρικανός/ Νοτιοαφρικανή	*noteea afreekee: noteeoafreekanos/ noteeoafreekanee*
United States: American	Ηνωμένες Πολιτείες: Αμερικανός/ Αμερικανίδα	*eenomenes poleeteees: amereekanos/ amereekaneedha*

sound check

Χ, χ sounds like the Scottish 'ch' in 'loch':
έχετε *ehete*

Practise on these words:
χρώμα *hr**o**ma* ευχαριστώ *ethareest**o***

try it out

question time

Match the questions on the left with the appropriate answers on the right.

1 Πού είναι το μουσείο;
2 Τι δουλειά κάνετε;
3 Πόσο χρονών είστε;
4 Πόσο κάνει αυτό;
5 Έχετε κάρτες;

a Είμαι νοσοκόμα.
b Μάλιστα.
c Αριστερά.
d Εβδομήντα λεπτά.
e Τριάντα πέντε.

as if you were there

On holiday in Greece, you get chatting to a man at a bar. Follow the prompts to play your part.

Γεια σου. Τι κάνεις;
(Say hello, you're very well, thank you)
Με λένε Δημήτρη. Εσένα πώς σε λένε?
(Say your name is Sarah)
Από πού είσαι;
(Say you are from Scotland, and you come from Edinburgh)

linkup

key phrases

Πού είναι η τράπεζα; *poo **ee**ne ee tr**a**peza*	**Where is** the bank?
Υπάρχει τηλέφωνο; *eep**a**rhee teel**e**fono*	**Is there** a telephone?
Υπάρχουν τουαλέτες; *eep**a**rhoon tooal**e**tes*	**Are there** any toilets?
Έχετε παγωτό; ***e**hete paghot**o***	**Do you have** any ice cream?
Θέλω εκατό γραμμάρια. *th**e**lo ekat**o** gramm**a**reea*	**I'd like** a hundred grammes.
Με λένε ... *me l**e**ne*	**My name is** ...
Είμαι Άγγλος/Αγγλίδα. ***ee**me **a**nglos/angl**ee**dha*	**I'm** English. (male/female)
Είμαι από το Λονδίνο. ***ee**me ap**o** to londh**ee**no*	**I'm from** London.
Έχω δύο παιδιά. ***e**ho dh**ee**o pedhee**a***	**I have** two children.

listening & replying

When people ask you questions about yourself, such as:
Έχετε οικογένεια; Do you have (any) family?
ehete eekoyeneea
it's tempting to reply using the same word: έχετε *ehete*.
But instead, you change the form of the verb, using
έχω (I have) not έχετε (you have):
Έχω δύο παιδιά. I have two children.
eho dheeo pedheea

missing words

Because the form of the verb tells you who is being referred to, it is very common not to use the words for 'I' (εγώ *egho*) or 'you' (εσύ/εσείς *esee/esees*) in Greek:

Είμαι Άγγλος. (not εγώ είμαι Άγγλος) I'm English.
eeme anglos (not *egho eeme anglos*)

'Εχετε παιδιά; (not εσείς έχετε παιδιά) Do you have any children?
ehete pedheea (not *esees ehete pedheea*)

The same applies to the words for 'he', 'she' and 'it': αυτός *aftos*, αυτή *aftee* and αυτό *afto*:

Πού είναι το μουσείο; – Είναι ίσια. (not αυτό είναι ίσια)
Where's the museum? – It's straight on.
poo eene to mooseeo – eene eeseea (not *afto eene eeseea*)

For more on these words, see the Language Builder, p137. ⇢

the way you say things

You can't always transfer things word for word from one language to another. For instance, Πώς σας λένε; *pos sas lene* literally means 'How do they call you?'.

So sometimes it pays to learn the whole phrase rather than the individual words.

Notice also that in Greek, you need a word for 'the' with place names:
Είμαι από το Λονδίνο. I'm from (the) London.
eeme apo to londheeno

For more advice on when to use 'the' in Greek, see the Language Builder, p133. ⇢

Getting **Around**

by air

For a small country, Greece has a surprising number of airports, with routes converging on Athens Airport, also known as Eleftherios Venizelos. Most international scheduled flights are to Athens and Thessaloniki, but regular flights also serve the main islands of Corfu, Crete (at Iraklion and Hania) and Rhodes. Charter flights go to other popular destinations – Samos, Zakynthos, Kavala (Thassos) and Santorini – during high season.

by coach

On major routes, **τα λεωφορεία** *ta leofor**ee**a* (coach) services are a reliable and inexpensive way to travel. The islands and even the remotest villages are covered by their network. On main routes, book a seat a few hours in advance at peak holiday times and weekends. Single tickets are the norm. See **www.ktel.org** for information and timetables.

The main Athens coach station is at Kifissou 100, for departures to the Peloponnese, western and northern Greece. For central Greece, go to the station at Liossion 260. In Thessaloniki the main KTEL office is on Giannitson 194, near the railway station.

by train

Train travel is reasonably priced, and increasingly efficient as the network undergoes major modernisation. At terminals you can reserve a seat in advance. Otherwise, hop on and try and find a seat; first class carriages tend to have more available and tickets are not too expensive.

The two main routes – Athens to Thessaloniki and Patra – offer express services. There is a supplement for travel on Intercity trains, where advance booking is advised. Sleeper trains cover Alexandroupoli to Thessaloniki and Athens. If you plan to make a lot of journeys, invest in a pass for 10, 20 or 30 days. For fares and timetables, see **www.ose.gr**.

city transport

The metro is the fastest and cheapest way to travel in and around Athens. Line 3 serves the airport, while a network of interconnections with the Προαστιακός *proasteeakos*, the tram network (serving southern coastal suburbs) and buses will take you all around the city.

Ask at ticket offices about the range of travel cards and discounts available. Always stamp your ticket in the special machines on entry or face a fine – spot checks are common. Remember that tickets to the airport cost more than single-journey tickets within the city.

by sea

The monthly ***Greek Travel Pages*** is the best source of boat times: **www.gtp.gr**. A timetable of all routes out of Piraeus (but not back) for the current week is available from the Greek National Tourist Organisation (EOT) office in Syntagma Square, Athens (**www.gnto.gr**) and the English language paper ***Athens News*** (**www.athensnews.gr**) also publishes weekly ferry schedules from Piraeus, Rafina and Lavrion.

Large ferry and hydrofoil facilities are generally good, though food outlets tend to have limited fare and opening hours. Vegetarians are advised to take their own supplies.

If time is a priority, you may want to take a hydrofoil or catamaran (also known as 'Flying Dolphin'), usually twice as fast – and expensive – as ferries. Subject to cancellation in very windy weather, they are not recommended for those prone to travel sickness, and should be booked in advance.

Except in high season, ferry foot passengers do not need to buy advance tickets unless a cabin is required. Basic 'deck passage' is cheap, but seats are scarce and overcrowding is common. If taking a car or motorbike, book in advance, online or from one of the numerous travel agents in Athens and around the country.

ferry ports

Paros and Naxos are the hub of the ferry system in the Aegean, with links to each other and also to Ios, Santorini, Mykonos, Crete, Sikinos, Folegandros and (in summer) Amorgos. Paros also links with Sifnos (summer only). The frequency of these links varies monthly. High season is July to early September.

Piraeus The main port for the Aegean islands, the nearby Saronic Gulf islands, the Cyclades, the Dodecanese, Crete and the Eastern Aegean.

Rafina To Andros and Tinos and as an alternative departure point to the Cyclades. Rafina is one hour's drive from Athens.

Patra To Kefalonia, Ithaki, Corfu and Italy. Patra is three hours from Athens by coach or Inter-city train.

Killini To Zakynthos.

Kavala, Macedonia To Thassos and Limnos.

Volos, Aghios Constantinos (summer only) To Skiathos, Skopelos and Alonissos.

Kimi, Evia To Skyros.

hydrofoil ports

Zea Marina, Athens For Crete and the main Cyclades islands, the main Saronic Gulf islands, Porto Heli (near Spetses) and the eastern Peloponnese. There is also a route serving Epidaurus, useful for the summer festival.

Aghios Constantinos, Volos and Thessaloniki For the Sporades islands.

Dodecanese islands connected from Rhodes - Kalymnos - Kos - Patmos - Symi - Tilos - Samos etc.

Ionian islands With links between: Zakynthos - Ithaki - Kefalonia and ports on the mainland and Albania.

car or bike hire

International car hire companies have offices in all airports and major towns. Numerous local companies operate (find them at **www.steea.gr**), but check what you are paying for and make sure you are properly insured.

Mopeds and bikes can be hired at most resorts at reasonable prices, and sometimes motorbikes if you hold a valid licence. Mopeds are a good way of getting around dirt roads, but take great care as accidents are all too common and you will have to pay for repairs (to yourself and the moped). Always check the brakes first.

driving in Greece

An ambitious upgrading programme means that the main roads linking major cities are being improved. However, many provincial roads are in fairly poor condition. **Εθνικές Οδοί** *ethneek**e**s od**ee*** (national roads) are good-quality toll roads which run from Athens to Corinth and Patra, Lamia and Thessaloniki, Thessaloniki to the border with Turkey etc.

Try to avoid entering or leaving Athens and Thessaloniki on a Friday afternoon or Sunday evening, when traffic is frequently reduced to a snail's pace. Central Athens is probably best avoided altogether. Legal parking spaces are restricted and, if you are in a hire car, you will be subject to the strict anti-pollution laws which prevent you from driving in the city centre before 5pm on alternate weekdays, the day being determined by your registration plate number. The police may remove the licence plates of illegally parked cars (effectively clamping them) and it will involve a hefty fine and lots of paperwork to get them back.

The accident toll in Greece is unacceptably high and the driving often fast and aggressive. Crete, in particular, has a reputation for this. Cars tend to overtake on either side, while a disproportionate number of accidents occur during the afternoon siesta time. Remember that flashing headlights mean 'Get out of the way!' not 'Come on!', and be careful on railway level crossings (often unguarded) and slippery surfaces in wet weather. Drink driving is dealt with severely by the police.

Petrol is cheap, but in rural areas petrol stations can be few and far between – don't let your tank get too low.

phrasemaker

finding the way

you may say ...

Excuse me ...	Συγνώμη ...	*seeghn**o**mee*
Is there ... near here?	Υπάρχει ... εδώ κοντά;	*eep**a**rhee ... edh**o** kond**a***
a chemist's	φαρμακείο	*farmak**ee**o*
a park	πάρκο	*p**a**rko*
an internet café	ίντερνετ καφέ	***ee**nternet kaf**e***
a tourist office	τουριστικό γραφείο	*tooreesteek**o** ghraf**ee**o*
a cash point	ATM (μηχάνημα ανάληψης μετρητών)	*ATM (meeh**a**neema an**a**leepsees metreet**o**n)*
a bus stop	στάση λεωφορείου	*st**a**see leofor**ee**oo*
a metro stop	στάση μετρό	*st**a**see metr**o***
Where is the nearest bank?	Πού είναι η πιο κοντινή τράπεζα;	*poo **ee**ne ee pee**o** kondeen**ee** tr**a**peza*
Is the ... far?	Είναι μακριά ...	***ee**ne makree**a***
church	η εκκλησία;	*ee eklees**ee**a*
station	ο σταθμός;	*o stathm**o**s*
port	το λιμάνι;	*to leem**a**nee*
Which way is the ...	Πού είναι ...	*poo **ee**ne*
information office?	οι πληροφορίες;	*ee pleerofor**ee**es*
coach station?	ο σταθμός λεωφορείων;	*o stathm**o**s leofor**ee**on*
Are there any ... near here?	Υπάρχουν ... εδώ κοντά;	*eep**a**rhoon ... edh**o** kond**a***
toilets	τουαλέτες	*tooal**e**tes*
large shops	μεγάλα καταστήματα	*megh**a**la katast**ee**mata*
Is this the right way to ...	Πάμε καλά για ...	*p**a**me kal**a** ya*
the train station?	το σταθμό τρένων;	*to stathm**o** tr**e**non*
the town centre?	το κέντρο της πόλης;	*to k**e**ndro tees p**o**lees*

How far is ...	Πόσο μακριά είναι ...	*p**o**so makree**a** **ee**ne*
the metro?	το μετρό;	*to metr**o***
the airport?	το αεροδρόμιο;	*to aerodhr**o**meeo*

you may hear ...

Είναι ...	***ee**ne*	It's ...
δεξιά.	*dhekse**ea***	on the right.
αριστερά.	*areester**a***	on the left.
μετά ίσια/ευθεία	*met**a** **ee**seea/efth**ee**a*	then straight on
σε εκατό μέτρα	*se ekat**o** m**e**tra*	100 metres away
στη γωνία	*stee ghon**ee**a*	on the corner
Είναι ...	***ee**ne*	It's ...
(αρκετά) κοντά.	*(arket**a**) kond**a***	(fairly) close.
(αρκετά) μακριά.	*(arket**a**) makree**a***	(fairly) far away.
απέναντι από ...	*ap**e**nandee ap**o***	opposite the ...
πίσω από ...	*p**ee**so ap**o***	behind the ...
Νάτος! (m)/Νάτη! (f)/ Νάτο! (n)	*n**a**tos/n**a**tee/ n**a**to*	There it is!
Στρίψτε ...	*str**ee**pste*	Turn ...
Περάστε ...	*per**a**ste*	Cross the ...
τη γέφυρα.	*tee y**e**feera*	bridge.
τον κύριο δρόμο.	*ton k**ee**reeo dhr**o**mo*	main road.
πρώτο/δεύτερο ...	*pr**o**to/dh**e**ftero*	first/second ...
Μέχρι την πλατεία.	*m**e**hree teen plat**ee**a*	As far as the square.
στο τέλος του δρόμου	*sto t**e**los too dhr**o**moo*	at the end of the street

(For a list of shops see p57, and for places to visit see p107.)

check out 1

You stop a passer-by to ask the way to the station.

❍ Συγνώμη, πού είναι ο σταθμός παρακαλώ;
*seeghn**o**mee poo **ee**ne o stathm**o**s parakal**o***

\- Ίσια, μετά δεξιά, μετά αριστερά και νάτος.
***ee**seea met**a** dhekse**ea** met**a** areester**a** ke n**a**tos*

❍ Ευχαριστώ πολύ.
*efhareest**o** pol**ee***

\- Παρακαλώ.
*parakal**o***

Q The station on the right: true or false?

hiring a car or bike

you may say ...

I'd like to hire a ...	Θέλω να νοικιάσω ...	*th**e**lo na neekee**a**so*
car.	ένα αυτοκίνητο.	***e**na aftok**ee**neeto*
bike.	ένα ποδήλατο.	***e**na podh**ee**lato*
motorbike.	μία μηχανή.	*m**ee**a meehan**ee***
a ...	ένα ...	***e**na*
small	μικρό	*meekr**o***
medium	μεγάλο	*megh**a**lo*
big	αρκετά μεγάλο	*arket**a** megh**a**lo*
for ...	για ...	*ya*
three days	τρεις μέρες	*trees m**e**res*
a week	μία εβδομάδα	*m**ee**a evdhom**a**dha*
the weekend	το Σαββατοκύριακο	*to savatok**ee**reeako*
How much is it ...	Πόσο κάνει ...	*p**o**so k**a**nee*
per day?	την ημέρα;	*teen eem**e**ra*
per week?	την εβδομάδα;	*teen evdhom**a**dha*
Is insurance included?	Περιλαμβάνεται η ασφάλεια;	*pereelamv**a**nete ee asf**a**leea*

you may hear ...

Το δίπλωμά σας παρακαλώ.	*to dh**ee**ploma sas parakal**o***	Your driving licence, please.
Για πόσο καιρό;	*ya poso ker**o***	For how long?
Κοστίζει ... την ημέρα.	*kost**ee**zee ... teen eemera*	It costs ... a day.

check out 2

You make enquiries about hiring a car.

- Θέλω να νοικιάσω ένα μικρό αυτοκίνητο.
  *thelo na neekeeaso ena meekr**o** aftok**ee**neeto*
- Έχουμε μόνο μεσαία.
  *ehoome m**o**no mese**a***
- Εντάξει.
  *end**a**ksee*
- Για πόσο καιρό;
  *ya poso ker**o***
- Για τρεις μέρες.
  *ya trees m**e**res*
- Το δίπλωμά σας παρακαλώ.
  *to dh**ee**ploma sas parakal**o***

(έχουμε = we have)

Q The car you took was a medium size: true or false?

on the road

you may say ...

Is this road to ...?	Αυτός ο δρόμος βγάζει στον/στην/στο ...;	*aft**o**s o dhr**o**mos vg**a**zee ston/steen/sto*
How far is it to ...?	Πόσο απέχει ...;	*p**o**so ap**e**hee*
Where is the car park?	Πού είναι το πάρκινγκ;	*poo **ee**ne to p**a**rkeeng*
Can I park here?	Μπορώ να παρκάρω εδώ;	*bor**o** na park**a**ro edh**o***

buying petrol

you may say ...

30 litres/€20 of unleaded.	Τριάντα λίτρα/Είκοσι ευρώ αμόλυβδη.	*treeanda leetra/ eekosee evro amoleevdhee*
Where is the ...	Πού είναι ...	*poo eene ee*
super unleaded?	η σούπερ αμόλυβδη;	*ee sooper amoleevdhee*
diesel?	το ντίζελ;	*to deezel*
Fill it up!	Γεμίστε το!	*yemeeste to*
Do you have any ...	Έχετε ...	*ehete*
air?	αέρα;	*aera*
water?	νερό;	*nero*
oil?	λάδι;	*ladhee*

road signs

you may see ...

Στάθμευση	Parking
Μονά/ζυγά	Odd/Even
Τηρήστε το δεξιό της οδού	Keep right
Ανάψτε τα φανάρια σας	Use lights
Προτεραιότητα	Priority
Ο δρόμος είναι κλειστός	No entry
Είσοδος	Entry
Έξοδος	Exit
Διόδια	Toll
Παράκαμψη	Diversion
Βορράς/Νότος	North/South

getting information

you may say ...

Is there a ... to ...?	Υπάρχει ... για ...;	*eeparhee ... ya*
ferry	φέρρυ μπόουτ	*feree booot*
train	τρένο	*treno*
boat	καράβι	*karavee*
hydrofoil	ιπτάμενο δελφίνι	*eeptameno dhelfeenee*
Does this train/bus go to ...	Αυτό το τρένο/ λεωφορείο πάει ...	*afto to treno/ leoforeeo paee*
Patra?	στην Πάτρα;	*steen Patra*
the airport?	στο αεροδρόμιο;	*sto aerodhromeeo*
What time does the bus for ... leave?	Τι ώρα φεύγει το λεωφορείο για ...;	*tee ora fevyee to leoforeeo ya*
What time does it arrive in ...?	Τι ώρα φτάνει στην ...;	*tee ora ftanee steen*
What time does the next one leave?	Τι ώρα φεύγει το επόμενο;	*tee ora fevyee to epomeno*
Which platform?	Από ποια πλατφόρμα;	*apo peea platforma*
How long does it take?	Πόση ώρα κάνει;	*posee ora kanee*
Have you got the timetable?	Έχετε το δρομολόγιο;	*ehete to dhromologheeo*
Can you tell me where to get off?	Πού πρέπει να κατέβω;	*poo prepee na katevo*
Do I have to change?	Πρέπει να αλλάξω;	*prepee nalakso*

you may hear ...

Κατεβείτε στον/στην ...	*kateveete ston/steen*	Get off at ...
Αλλάξτε στον/στην ...	*alakste ston/steen*	Change at ...
Θα σας δείξω.	*tha sas dheekso*	I'll show you.
Στις δέκα το πρωί.	*stees deka to proee*	At 10 o'clock in the morning. (See times, p16)

check out 3

You want to take the train to Thessaloniki.

- ❍ Τι ώρα φεύγει το τρένο για τη Θεσσαλονίκη;
  *tee **o**ra f**e**vgee to tr**e**no ya tee thesalon**ee**kee*
- \- Στις οχτώ το πρωί.
  *stees oht**o** to pro**ee***
- ❍ Και τι ώρα φτάνει;
  *ke tee **o**ra ft**a**nee*
- \- Στις δύο.
  *stees dh**ee**o*

(πρωί = morning)

Q What time does the train leave?
What time does it arrive?

buying a ticket

you may say ...

Where is the ticket office please?	Πού είναι το εκδοτήριο παρακαλώ;	*poo **ee**ne to ekdhot**ee**reeo parakal**o***
A ticket to ..., please.	Ένα εισιτήριο για ..., παρακαλώ.	***e**na eeseet**ee**reeo ya parakal**o***
I'd like ...	Θέλω ...	*th**e**lo*
a single.	ένα απλό.	***e**na apl**o***
a return.	ένα με επιστροφή.	***e**na me epeestrof**ee***
a day travel card.	μία ημερήσια κάρτα.	*m**ee**a eemer**ee**seea k**a**rta*
two tickets.	δύο εισιτήρια.	*dh**ee**o eeseet**ee**reea*
for two adults and one child	δύο κανονικά και ένα παιδικό	*dh**ee**o kanoneek**a** ke **e**na pedheek**o***
first/second class	πρώτη/δεύτερη θέση	*pr**o**tee/dh**e**fteree th**e**see*
I'd like to reserve a ...	θέλω να κλείσω μία ...	*th**e**lo na kl**ee**so m**ee**a*
seat.	θέση.	*th**e**see*
couchette.	κουκέτα.	*kook**e**ta*
cabin.	καμπίνα.	*kab**ee**na*
Is there a reduction for ...	Υπάρχει μειωμένο για ...	*eep**a**rhee meeom**e**no ya*
students?	φοιτητές;	*feeteet**e**s*
senior citizens?	συνταξιούχους;	*seendaksee**oo**hoos*
Is there wheelchair access?	Υπάρχει πρόσβαση για άτομα με αναπηρίες;	*eep**a**rhee pr**o**zvasee ya **a**toma me anapeer**ee**es*

you may hear ...

Καπνίζοντες ή μη καπνίζοντες;	*kapn**ee**zondes ee mee kapn**ee**zondes*	Smoking or non-smoking?
Υπάρχει επιβάρυνση.	*eep**a**rhee epeev**a**reensee*	There is a supplement.
Μπορείτε ν' αγοράσετε εισιτήριο στο τρένο.	*bor**ee**te naghor**a**sete eeseet**ee**reeo sto tr**e**no*	You can buy a ticket on the train.

check out 4

You are buying tickets for you and two friends to travel to Spetses by hydrofoil.

❍ Τρία εισιτήρια με το Δελφίνι για τις Σπέτσες, παρακαλώ.
*tr**ee**a eeseet**ee**reea me to dhelf**ee**nee ya tees sp**e**tses, parakal**o***

\- Απλά ή με επιστροφή;
*apl**a** ee me epeestrof**ee***

❍ Απλά.
*apl**a***

\- Εξήντα ευρώ, παρακαλώ.
*eks**ee**nda evr**o** parakal**o***

❍ Ορίστε.
*or**ee**ste*

Q You are asked when you want to travel: true or false?
What's the total cost?

signs

you may see ...

Αφίξεις	Arrivals
Αναχωρήσεις	Departures
Αποβάθρα/πλατφόρμα	Platform
Ακυρώστε το εισιτήριό σας	Validate your ticket
Φύλαξη αποσκευών	Left luggage

taking a taxi

you may say ...

Is there a taxi rank near here?	Υπάρχει πιάτσα ταξί εδώ κοντά;	*eeparhee peeatsa taksee edho konta*
To the airport, please.	Στο αεροδρόμιο, παρακαλώ.	*sto aerodhromeeo parakalo*
To this address, please.	Πάω σ' αυτή τη διεύθυνση, παρακαλώ.	*pao saftee tee dheeeftheensee parakalo*
How long till we get there?	Σε πόση ώρα θα είμαστε εκεί;	*se posee ora tha eemaste ekee*
Is it far?	Είναι μακρυά;	*eene makreea*
How much is it/will it be?	Πόσο κάνει;	*poso kanee*
Keep the change.	Κρατείστε τα ρέστα.	*krateeste ta resta*
This is for you.	Ορίστε.	*oreeste*
Can I have a receipt, please?	Μου δίνετε μία απόδειξη, παρακαλώ;	*moo dheenete meea apodheeksee parakalo*

you may hear ...

γύρω στα είκοσι λεπτά	*yeero sta eekosee lepta*	about 20 minutes
Είναι ...	*eene*	It's ...
πολύ κοντά.	*polee konda*	very near.
αρκετά μακρυά.	*arketa makreea*	quite far.

sound check

Y, υ is sometimes pronounced like a 'v':

φεύγει *f**e**vyee* — αύριο ***a**vreeo*

but after the letters **α** and **ε** it sounds like an 'f':

ευχαριστώ *efhareest**o*** — ευθεία *efth**ee**a*

Practise on these words:

ευρώ *evr**o*** — αυτοκίνητο *aftok**ee**neeto*

try it out

mind the gap

Find the missing words. Then put their first letters together to make the word for a type of public transport.

1 'Small' _ _ _ _ _
2 'Thank you' _ _ _ _ _ _ _ _ _ _
3 _ _ ώρα φεύγει το λεωφορείο;
4 Κρατείστε τα _ _ _ _ _
5 'This is for you' _ _ _ _ _ _

as if you were there

Imagine you're in the station, finding out about trains to Pyrghos (Πύργο). Follow the prompts to play your part.

(Ask what time the train to Pyrghos leaves)
Οχτώ και τριάντα το πρωί.
(Ask how long it takes to Pyrghos)
Οχτώ ώρες.
(Ask if you need to change)
Ναι, στην Πάτρα.
(Ask for two return tickets)

linkup

Πού είναι ο σταθμός; *poo **ee**ne o stathm**o**s*	**Where's** the station?
Υπάρχει τράπεζα **εδώ κοντά**; *eep**a**rhee tr**a**peza edh**o** kond**a***	**Is there** a bank **near here**?
Έχετε χάρτη της πόλης; ***e**hete h**a**rtee tees p**o**lees*	**Do you have** a map of the town?
Θέλω να νοικιάσω ένα αυτοκίνητο. *th**e**lo na neekee**a**so **e**na aftok**ee**neeto.*	**I want to** hire a car.
Τι ώρα φεύγει το λεωφορείο; *tee **o**ra f**e**vyee to leofor**ee**o*	**What time** does the bus leave?
Μπορώ να παρκάρω εδώ; *bor**o** na park**a**ro edh**o***	**Can I** park here?

how to ask a question

In Greek a question mark is denoted by a sign that looks like our semicolon: **;**

A simple way to ask questions that do not include a question word (who?, when? etc.) is to use a statement and adjust the intonation, so that your voice rises towards the end of the phrase:

Μπορώ να παρκάρω εδώ. I can park here.
*bor**o** na park**a**ro edh**o***

Μπορώ να παρκάρω εδώ; Can I park here?
*bor**o** na park**a**ro edh**o***

Notice how Greek has no equivalent of the English use of 'do' or 'does' in questions.

Τι ώρα φτάνει το λεωφορείο; What time does the bus arrive?
*tee **o**ra ft**a**nee to leofor**ee**o* (literally, What time arrives the bus?)

Some handy question words:
Πόσο; *poso* How much?
Πότε; *pote* When?
Τι; *tee* What?
Πού; *poo* Where?
Πώς; *pos* How?

For more on asking questions, see the Language Builder, pp137-138. ⇢

words for 'the' & 'a'

In Greek there are different words for 'a', 'an' and 'the':
η τράπεζα the bank
ee trapeza
but **ο** σταθμός the station
o stathmos
ένα εισιτήριο a/one ticket
ena eeseeteereeo
but **μία** θέση a/one seat
meea thesee
This is because in Greek, words for things are either masculine, feminine or neuter. These three groups are known as 'genders'.

The word for 'the' is **ο** for a singular masculine word, **η** for a singular feminine word and **το** for a singular neuter word.

The word for 'a' or 'an' is ένας *enas* for a masculine word, μία *meea* for a feminine word and ένα *ena* for a neuter word.

For more about gender, see the Language Builder, p132. ⇢

Somewhere **to Stay**

The Greek National Tourist board (EOT) has lists of different types of accommodation, from hotels and campsites to self-catering apartments or farmhouses. Visit local offices, or look online: **www.gnto.gr** or **www.eot.gr**.

hotels

In principal resorts and towns, hotels are open all year round. The star rating system applies, however you may still find information on hotels using the old EOT system. At the top of the range is the 'luxury' category (five-star); at the bottom is E class (one-star). Controls exist on prices in all categories and prices should be displayed on the back of room doors. Note that in smaller and more remote resorts, many hotels close for the winter, usually from November to April. Most will offer breakfast and some can offer half or full board. Most hotels cater for children, and cots can usually be supplied if requested in advance.

historic buildings

The EOT renovates historical buildings and lets them out as 'Traditional Guesthouses' or 'Settlements'. These allow you to stay in comfort in some great locations, from tower houses in the Mani (Areopoli and Vathia) to the beautiful mansions of Pelion's villages, as well as in Koryschades in central Greece and on Psara near Chios.

rooms & guesthouses

In the summer, there are thousands of **δωμάτια** *domateea* (rooms) available across the country, officially graded by EOT. From November to early April, almost all rooms close down. In rooms and **πανσιόν** *panseeon* (guesthouses) it is worth bargaining over the room price. This can secure a reduction of up to a third, particularly if you plan to stay more than one night. Prices peak in July and August.

Rooms can be inside a family home, and range from the very basic, with just a sink and separate toilet, to those with private bathroom and cooking facilities. Breakfast is rarely offered.

youth hostels

Found in all cities and major towns, as well as on the islands of Crete, Santorini and Corfu, and main tourist destinations such as Mount Olympus and Delphi, these tend to be basic, and sometimes require an HI Card. Additionally, Athens has a number of Student Hostels (open to everyone) offering a cheap bed for the night.

self-catering

Most islands and resorts have a range of self-catering villas and apartments available. The former are usually let by the week. Best booked by a travel agent in advance, these can also be found via the local tourist office.

Remember that food supplies on some of the more out-of-the-way islands can be limited, and a car may be needed if you're based in one of the more remote areas.

camping

There are hundreds of campsites around the country, varying considerably in size and range of facilities. Some are open all year round. To find a campsite, try **www.campingreece.gr**.

Camping is generally very safe and open to camper vans, though only a few cater for the disabled. Camping in the wild is technically illegal, although not uncommon.

phrasemaker

places to stay

you may say …

campsite	κάμπινγκ	*k**a**mpeeng*
hotel	ξενοδοχείο	*ksenodhoh**ee**o*
pension	πανσιόν	*pansee**o**n*
rooms	δωμάτια	*dhom**a**teea*
beds	κρεβάτια	*krev**a**teea*
youth hostel	ξενώνας νεότητας	*ksen**o**nas ne**o**teetas*
self-catering	διαμερίσματα με κουζίνα	*dheeamer**ee**zmata me kooz**ee**na*
apartments to let	ενοικιάζονται διαμερίσματα	*eneekee**a**zonte dheeamer**ee**zmata*

finding a place & checking in

you may say …

I have a reservation ...	Έχω κλείσει ...	***e**ho kl**ee**see*
My name's ...	Λέγομαι ...	*l**e**ghome*
Is there a campsite near here?	Υπάρχει κάμπινγκ εδώ κοντά;	*eep**a**rhee k**a**mpeeng edh**o** kond**a***
Do you have a ... room?	Έχετε ... δωμάτιο;	***e**hete ... dhom**a**teeo*
single	μονόκλινο	*mon**o**kleeno*
double	δίκλινο	*dh**ee**kleeno*
triple	τρίκλινο	*tr**ee**kleeno*
for ...	για ...	*ya*
one/two nights	μία/δύο βραδιές	*m**ee**a/dh**ee**o vradhe**e**s*
one/two weeks	μία/δύο εβδομάδες	*m**ee**a/dh**ee**o evdhom**a**dhes*
four people	τέσσερα άτομα	*t**e**sera **a**toma*
two adults and two children	δύο μεγάλους και δύο παιδιά	*dh**ee**o megh**a**lous ke dh**ee**o pedh**ee**a*

with ... a bathroom a shower	με ... μπάνιο ντους	*me* *b**a**neeo* *doos*
with a single/double bed	με μονό/διπλό κρεβάτι	*me mon**o**/dheepl**o** krev**a**tee*
May I see the room?	Μπορώ να δω το δωμάτιο;	*bor**o** na dho to dhom**a**teeo*
How much is it ... per night? per week?	Πόσο κοστίζει ... τη βραδιά; την εβδομάδα;	*p**o**so kost**ee**zee* *tee vradhee**a*** *teen evdhom**a**dha*
Do you have anything cheaper?	Έχετε κάτι φθηνότερο;	***e**hete k**a**tee ftheen**o**tero*
Is there wheelchair access?	Υπάρχει πρόσβαση για άτομα με αναπηρίες;	*eep**a**rhee pr**o**zvasee ya **a**toma me anapeer**ee**es*
I'll take it.	Θα το πάρω.	*tha to p**a**ro*
We'll think about it.	Θα το σκεφτούμε.	*tha to skeft**oo**me*

you may hear ...

Το όνομά σας, παρακαλώ.	*to **o**nom**a** sas parakal**o***	Your name, please.
Πόσες βραδιές;	*p**o**ses vradhee**e**s*	How many nights?
Για πόσα άτομα;	*ya p**o**sa **a**toma*	For how many people?
Συγνώμη, είμαστε γεμάτοι.	*seeghn**o**mee **ee**maste yem**a**tee*	I'm sorry, we're full.
Τα παιδιά μισοτιμής.	*ta pedhee**a** meesoteem**ee**s*	Children half price.
Το διαβατήριό σας, παρακαλώ.	*to dheeavat**ee**ree**o** sas parakal**o***	Your passport, please.
Παρακαλώ, συμπληρώστε το έντυπο.	*parakal**o** seembleer**o**ste to **e**ndeepo*	Please fill in the form.
Αριθμός δωματίου ...	*areethm**o**s dhomat**ee**oo*	Room number ...
Ποιος είναι ο αριθμός του αυτοκινήτου σας;	*pee**o**s **ee**ne o areethm**o**s too aftokeen**ee**too sas*	What is your car registration?

Somewhere to **Stay**

check out 1

You are enquiring about renting a double room on an island.

❍ Καλημέρα σας. Έχετε δίκλινο δωμάτιο;
*kaleem**e**ra sas. **e**hete dh**ee**kleeno dhom**a**teeo*

\- Μάλιστα. Πόσες βραδιές;
*m**a**leesta. p**o**ses vradhee**e**s*

❍ Τρεις. Πόσο κοστίζει τη βραδιά;
*trees. p**o**so kost**ee**zee tee vradhee**a***

\- Σαράντα ευρώ.
*sar**a**nda evr**o***

❍ Έχετε κάτι φθηνότερο;
***e**hete k**a**tee ftheen**o**tero*

\- Μάλιστα. Είκοσι ευρώ χωρίς μπάνιο.
*m**a**leesta. **ee**kosee evr**o** hor**ee**s b**a**neeo*

❍ Εντάξει. Θα το πάρω.
*end**a**ksee. tha to p**a**ro*

(χωρίς = without)

Q How much is the cheaper room?
Does it have a bathroom?

asking about your room

you may say ...

Does the room have ...	Έχει το δωμάτιο ...	*ehee to dhomat**ee**o*
a shower?	ντους;	*doos*
a bath?	μπάνιο;	*b**a**neeo*
(satellite) TV?	(δορυφορική) τηλεόραση;	*(dhoreeforeek**ee**) teele**o**rasee*
an internet connection?	σύνδεση ίντερνετ;	*s**ee**ndhesee **ee**nternet*
a balcony?	μπαλκόνι;	*balk**o**nee*

Is there a surcharge for the internet?	Υπάρχει επιβάρυνση για το ίντερνετ;	*eep**a**rhee epeev**a**reensee ya to **ee**nternet*
Is there ... a lift? room service?	Υπάρχει ... ασανσέρ; υπηρεσία δωματίων;	*eep**a**rhee* *asans**e**r* *eepeeres**ee**a dhomat**ee**on*
Where is ... the restaurant? the bar? the gym?	Πού είναι ... το εστιατόριο; το μπαρ; το γυμναστήριο;	*poo **ee**ne* *to esteeat**o**reeo* *to bar* *to yeemnast**ee**reeo*
How do I get an outside number?	Πώς παίρνω εξωτερική γραμμή;	*pos p**e**rno eksotereek**ee** ghram**ee***
Is breakfast included?	Περιλαμβάνεται το πρωινό;	*pereelamv**a**nete to proeen**o***
What time is breakfast?	Τι ώρα είναι το πρωινό;	*tee **o**ra **ee**ne to proeen**o***

you may hear ...

Δυστυχώς όχι.	*dheesteeh**o**s **o**hee*	Unfortunately not.
Το πρωινό σερβίρεται από τις ... μέχρι τις ...	*to proeen**o** serv**ee**rete ap**o** tees ... m**e**hree tees ...*	Breakfast is from ... to ...

Το πρωινό/ Ο φόρος ... περιλαμβάνεται. δεν περιλαμβάνεται.	*to proeen**o**/ o f**o**ros pereelamv**a**nete dhen pereelamv**a**nete*	Breakfast/Tax ... is included. not included.
Είναι στον τρίτο όροφο.	***ee**ne ston tr**ee**to **o**rofo*	It's on the third floor.
Πάρτε το μηδέν.	*p**a**rte to meedh**e**n*	Dial zero.
Χρειάζεστε αφύπνιση;	*hree**a**zeste af**ee**pneesee*	Do you want a wake up call?
Τι ώρα;	*tee **o**ra*	(For) what time?

check out 2

You are checking in with a reservation.

- Έχω κλείσει ένα μονόκλινο.
  *eho kl**ee**see **e**na mon**o**kleeno*
- Το όνομά σας, παρακαλώ.
  *to **o**noma sas parakal**o***
- Ελένη Οικονόμου.
  *el**e**nee eekon**o**moo*
- Το διαβατήριό σας, παρακαλώ.
  *to dheeavat**ee**reeo sas parakal**o***
- Ορίστε.
  *or**ee**ste*
- Ο αριθμός δωματίου είναι διακόσια τριάντα.
  *o areethm**o**s dhomat**ee**oo **ee**ne dheeak**o**seea tree**a**nda*

Q You are asked for your name and passport: true or false? What is your room number?

asking for help

you may say ...

Could I have an alarm call at ...?	Μπορείτε να με ξυπνήσετε στις ...;	*bor**ee**te na me kseepn**ee**sete stees*
Have you got a safe deposit box?	Έχετε θυρίδα;	***e**hete theer**ee**dha*
Do you have a map of the town?	Έχετε χάρτη της πόλης;	***e**hete h**a**rtee tees p**o**lees*
Could you ...	Μπορείτε να ...	*bor**ee**te na*
recommend a restaurant?	μου συστήσετε ένα εστιατόριο;	*moo seest**ee**sete **e**na esteeat**o**reeo*
order me a taxi?	καλέσετε ένα ταξί;	*kal**e**sete **e**na taks**ee***
Is there somewhere to park?	Μπορώ να παρκάρω κάπου;	*bor**o** na park**a**ro k**a**poo*
The ... isn't working.	Το ... δεν δουλεύει.	*to ... dhen dhool**e**vee*
telephone	τηλέφωνο	*teel**e**fono*
television	τηλεόραση	*teele**o**rasee*
light	φως	*fos*
How do you work ...	Πώς λειτουργεί ...	*pos leetoorgh**ee***
the shower?	το ντους;	*to doos*
the air conditioning?	το αιρ κοντίσιον;	*to er kond**ee**seeon*
the heating?	η θέρμανση;	*ee th**e**rmansee*
Do you have an iron?	Έχετε σίδερο;	***e**hete s**ee**dero*
There is no ...	Δεν έχει ...	*dhen **e**hee*
soap.	σαπούνι.	*sap**oo**nee*
(cold/hot) water.	(κρύο/ζεστό) νερό.	*(kr**ee**o/zest**o**) ner**o***
toilet paper.	χαρτί τουαλέτας.	*hart**ee** tooal**e**tas*
There are no ...	Δεν έχει ...	*dhen **e**hee*
towels.	πετσέτες.	*pets**e**tes*
pillows.	μαξιλάρια.	*makseel**a**reea*
blankets.	κουβέρτες.	*koov**e**rtes*
... is dirty.	... είναι βρώμικα.	*... **ee**ne vr**o**meeka*
The toilet	Η τουαλέτα	*ee tooal**e**ta*
The bathroom	Το μπάνιο	*to b**a**neeo*
The sheets are dirty.	Τα σεντόνια είναι βρώμικα.	*ta send**o**neea **ee**ne vr**o**meeka*

you may hear ...

Θα στείλουμε κάποιον.	*tha st**ee**loome k**a**peeon*	We'll send somebody.
Θα σας φέρω.	*tha sas f**e**ro*	I'll get you some.

check out 3

You are requesting an alarm call and making enquiries about breakfast in your hotel.

○ Μπορείτε να με ξυπνήσετε αύριο το πρωί;
*bor**ee**te na me kseepn**ee**sete **a**vreeo to pro**ee***

\- Μάλιστα. Τι ώρα θέλετε;
*m**a**leesta. tee **o**ra th**e**lete*

○ Στις έξι. Τι ώρα είναι το πρωινό;
*stees **e**ksee. tee **o**ra **ee**ne to proeen**o***

\- Το πρωινό σερβίρεται από τις εφτά και τριάντα μέχρι τις δέκα και τριάντα.
*to proeen**o** serv**ee**rete ap**o** tees eft**a** ke tree**a**nda m**e**hree tees dh**e**ka ke tree**a**nda*

○ Πού είναι το εστιατόριο;
*poo **ee**ne to esteeat**o**reeo*

\- Στον τρίτο όροφο.
*ston tr**ee**to **o**rofo*

Q What time will the receptionist wake you up?
Breakfast is served from 7.30 to 9.30am: true or false?

checking out

you may say ...

I'd like to pay the bill.	Θέλω να πληρώσω το λογαριασμό.	*the**l**o na pleer**o**so to loghareeazm**o***
by ...	με ...	*me*
travellers cheque	ταξιδιωτική επιταγή	*takseedheeoteek**ee** epeetay**ee***
credit card	πιστωτική κάρτα	*peestoteek**ee** k**a**rta*
cash	μετρητά	*metreet**a***
I think there is a mistake.	Νομίζω ότι υπάρχει κάποιο λάθος.	*nom**ee**zo **o**tee eep**a**rhee k**a**peeo l**a**thos*

you may hear ...

Ποιον αριθμό δωματίου;	*pee**o**n areethm**o** dhomat**ee**oo*	Which room number?
Πώς θα πληρώσετε;	*pos tha pleer**o**sete*	How will you pay?
Υπογράψτε εδώ.	*eepoghr**a**pste edh**o***	Sign here.

at the campsite

you may say ...

Have you got space for ...	Έχετε χώρο για ...	***e**hete h**o**ro ya*
a car?	ένα αυτοκίνητο;	***e**na aftok**ee**neeto*
a caravan?	ένα τροχόσπιτο;	***e**na troh**o**speeto*
a tent?	μια σκηνή;	*m**ee**a skeen**ee***
How much does it cost?	Πόσο κοστίζει;	*p**o**so kost**ee**zee*
Where are ...	Πού είναι ...	*poo **ee**ne*
the showers?	τα ντους;	*ta doos*
the dustbins?	οι σκουπιδοντενεκέδες;	*ee skoopeedhodenek**e**hes*
the toilets?	οι τουαλέτες;	*ee tooal**e**tes*
the electricity?	η παροχή ηλεκτρικού;	*ee paroh**ee** elektreek**oo***
Is there ...	Υπάρχει ...	*eep**a**rhee*
a laundry?	πλυντήριο;	*pleend**ee**reeo*
a shop?	μαγαζί;	*maghaz**ee***
a pool?	πισίνα;	*peeseena*

you may hear ...

Πόσο θα μείνετε;	*poso tha meenete*	How long are you going to stay?
Πόσα άτομα;	*posa atoma*	How many people?

check out 4

You are trying to find a space at a campsite.

- ❍ Γεια σας. Έχετε χώρο για ένα τροχόσπιτο;
  ya sas. ehete horo ya ena trohospeeto
- \- Συγνώμη. Είμαστε γεμάτοι.
  seeghnomee. eemaste yematee
- ❍ Υπάρχει άλλο κάμπινγκ εδώ κοντά;
  eeparhee alo kampeeng edho konda
- \- Μάλιστα. Στα Λουτρά.
  maleesta. sta lootra

Q Where is there an alternative campsite?

self-catering

you may say ...

I'd like to rent a villa.	Θέλω να νοικιάσω μια βίλλα.	*thelo na neekeeaso meea veela*
How does ... work? the heating the water	Πώς λειτουργεί ... το καλοριφέρ; το νερό;	*pos leetooryee* *to kaloreefer* *to nero*
When are the dustbins emptied?	Πότε μαζεύουν τα σκουπίδια;	*pote mazevoon ta skoopeedheea*

sound check

Ψ, ψ isn't equivalent to an English letter, but is pronounced like the 'ps' at the end of 'perhaps':

υπογράψτε *eepoghrapste* ψάρι *psaree*
ψωμί *psomee*

try it out

match it up

Match the Greek word with the correct type of accommodation.

1	διαμερίσματα	**a**	campsite
2	πανσιόν	**b**	hotel
3	κρεβάτια	**c**	pension
4	κάμπινγκ	**d**	rooms
5	δωμάτια	**e**	beds
6	ξενοδοχείο	**f**	apartments

Somewhere to **Stay**

in the mix

Correct the word order of each sentence to make a coversation at a hotel reception.

- Σας καλημέρα.
• Κλείσει έχω μονόκλινο ένα.
- Όνομά σας παρακαλώ το.
• Σμιθ Τζον.
- Το παρακαλώ σας διαβατήριό.
• Ορίστε!
- Το αυτό συμπληρώστε έντυπο.

as if you were there

Imagine you're in a hotel reception, asking about a room. Follow the prompts to play your part.

Καλημέρα.

(Say hello and ask if there are any double rooms available)

Μάλιστα. Με μπάνιο;

(Say yes and ask how much it costs per night)

Τριάντα ευρώ τη βραδιά. Πόσες βραδιές;

(Say two nights)

linkup

key phrases

Έχετε δίκλινο δωμάτιο; — **Do you have** a double room?
ehete dheekleeno dhomateeo

Πού είναι το εστιατόριο; — **Where's** the restaurant?
*poo **ee**ne to esteeat**o**reeo*

Δεν έχει σαπούνι. — **There isn't any** soap.
*dhen **e**hee sap**oo**nee*

Δεν δουλεύει η τηλεόραση. — The television **is not working**.
*dhen dool**e**vee ee teele**o**rasee*

Μπορείτε να καλέσετε ένα ταξί; — **Can you** call a taxi?
*bor**ee**te na kal**e**sete **e**na taks**ee***

negatives

To make a phrase negative, put δεν *dhen* meaning 'not', before the verb:

Δεν έχουμε μονόκλινο δωμάτιο. We don't have a single room.
dhen ehoome monokleeno dhomateeo

Δεν θέλω ταξί. I don't want a taxi.
dhen thelo taksee

For more on negatives, see the Language Builder, p138.

describing things

The words **δίκλινο** *dheekleeno* (double), **μονόκλινο** *monokleeno* (single), **μεγάλο** *meghalo* (large) are known as adjectives or describing words.

Just as the words for 'a' and 'the' change according to the gender of the word they describe, so too do adjectives. Many adjectives in Greek end in **-ο** or **-η**:

ένα δίκλινο δωμάτιο a double room (δωμάτιο is neuter, so you use the neuter form of the adjective: δίκλινο)

η μεγάλη πισίνα a swimming pool (πισίνα is feminine, so you use the feminine form of the adjective: μεγάλη)

The masculine form of the adjective (much less common than the others because there are relatively few masculine words) ends in **-ος**:

ο πρώτος όροφος the first floor (you use the masculine form of the word πρώτος because όροφος is masculine)

For more on adjectives, see the Language Builder, pp134-135.

Buying **Things**

shops

Shopping hours are complicated by seasonal variations and the fact that different types of shops have different hours. As a general rule, shops open from 9am to 2.30pm (Monday to Friday), and re-open on Tuesday, Thursday and Friday from about 5.30 to 8.30pm. On Saturday they open from 9am until 3pm. Exceptions to this are supermarkets, department stores and souvenir shops, which stay open throughout the day and, in resorts, on Sunday as well. Credit cards are accepted by large shops and department stores.

One of the most useful Greek shops is the **περίπτερο** *pereeptero* (kiosk), which acts as a newsagent's, tobacconist's and general store, and also sells stamps and phonecards.

Banks open Monday to Friday from 8am to 2pm. Airports have bank branches open every day from 8am to 7pm on weekdays and 9am to 4pm on Saturday, Sunday and Bank Holidays.

buying food

Permanent markets can be found in all main provincial towns and are recommended for good-quality, fresh produce. In Athens, the atmospheric central food markets are all on Athinas Street; in Thessaloniki, head for the Modiano. Additionally, most areas have a weekly fruit and vegetable **λαϊκή** *laeekee* (street market).

You may want to take home some honey, olives or olive oil (Kalamata and Amfissa are the best-known regions) or saffron from Kozani, in northern Greece. In many villages there are women's co-operatives selling homemade preserves, sauces, pasta, fruit liqueurs and other delicacies.

Supermarkets and mini-markets are everywhere and should cover most of your food needs. However, if you are travelling with a baby, bring some food supplies with you and remember that some baby formula is sold at chemists'.

buying souvenirs

Athens has many souvenir shops in the area around Plaka. At Yousouroum, the Sunday flea market, you can bargain for anything from clothes and music to art and crafts. Unofficially, you can also bargain in many of the regular shops in the area; a few words of Greek will definitely be to your advantage! The Sunday flea market in Piraeus and the bazaar area of Thessaloniki are also good for souvenirs. Look out for the many eye-shaped charms – a piece of jewellery designed to ward off evil wishes.

crafts

Jewellery Greece can be a relatively cheap place to buy jewellery. Voukourestiou Street in Athens is good for international designers, while Ioannina in Epirus is renowned for its silverwork.

Handwoven rugs and fabrics Look out for attractive, colourful textiles in Santorini, Naxos, Corfu and Skopelos. In Metsovo, Epirus, traditional weaving methods are still used, while φλοκάτες *flokates* rugs and handwoven bags are a speciality of Arachova. Crete has lovely, bright handwoven fabrics.

Embroidery A cottage industry on many islands, such as Naxos, Santorini, Lefkada and Skyros.

Pottery and ceramics As well as the tourist wares, you can find attractive, good value ceramics throughout the Cyclades.

Wood carvings Traditional techniques are practised in areas like Crete, Arcadia in the Peloponnese, and Lesvos, Ioannina. Look out for olive wood carvings in Corfu and wooden stools in Skyros.

Metalwork Look out for copper goods in Skyros, brass bells in Epirus, bronze handicraft in Thessalia and knives in Crete.

Buying Things

phrasemaker

general shopping phrases

you may say …

Do you have any …	Μήπως έχετε …	m**ee**pos **e**hete
cheese?	τυρί;	teer**ee**
jeans?	τζιν;	dseen
stamps?	γραμματόσημα;	ghramat**o**seema
English newspapers?	αγγλικές εφημερίδες;	angleek**e**s efeemer**ee**dhes
matches?	σπίρτα;	sp**ee**rta
… please.	… παρακαλώ.	… parakal**o**
A magazine	Ένα περιοδικό	**e**na pereeodheek**o**
A phone card	Μία κάρτα τηλεφώνου	m**ee**a kart**a** teelef**o**noo
A map of town	Ένα χάρτη	**e**na h**a**rtee
A lighter	Έναν αναπτήρα	**e**nan anapt**ee**ra
How much …	Πόσο …	p**o**so
is it?	κάνει;	k**a**nee
are they?	κάνουν;	k**a**noun
this one/that one	αυτό/εκείνο	aft**o**/ek**ee**no
What's that, please?	Τι είναι αυτό, παρακαλώ;	tee **ee**ne aft**o** parak**a**lo
How much is …	Πόσο κάνει …	p**o**so k**a**nee
the wine?	το κρασί;	to kras**ee**
the chocolate?	η σοκολάτα;	ee sokol**a**ta
How much are …	Πόσο κάνουν …	p**o**so k**a**noon
the CDs?	τα CD;	ta see dee
the postcards?	οι κάρτες;	ee k**a**rtes
the cigarettes?	τα τσιγάρα;	ta tseegh**a**ra
the sweets?	οι καραμέλες;	ee karam**e**les
That's all, thanks.	Αυτά, ευχαριστώ.	aft**a** efhareest**o**
How much is it altogether?	Πόσο κάνουν όλα μαζί;	p**o**so k**a**noon **o**la maz**ee**
Can I pay by credit card?	Μπορώ να πληρώσω με πιστωτική κάρτα;	bor**o** na pleer**o**so me peestoteek**ee** k**a**rta

you may hear ...

Να σας βοηθήσω;	*na sas voeeth**ee**so*	Can I help you?
Τι θα θέλατε;	*tee tha th**e**late*	What would you like?
Ορίστε.	*or**ee**ste*	Here you are.
Δυστυχώς όχι.	*dheesteeh**o**s **o**hee*	I'm afraid not.
Έχουμε μόνο ...	***e**hoome m**o**no*	We've only got ...
Παρακαλώ.	*parakal**o***	You're welcome.
Τίποτ' άλλο;	*t**ee**pot **a**lo*	Anything else?
Όλα μαζί πέντε ευρώ.	***o**la maz**ee** p**e**nde evr**o***	That's €5 altogether.

check out 1

You want to buy a phone card from a kiosk.

○ Τι θα θέλατε;
*tee tha th**e**late*

\- Μία κάρτα τηλεφώνου και δύο σοκολάτες, παρακαλώ.
*m**ee**a k**a**rta teelef**o**noo ke dh**ee**o sokol**a**tes parak**a**lo*

○ Ορίστε.
*or**ee**ste*

\- Μήπως έχετε γραμματόσημα;
*m**ee**pos **e**hete ghramat**o**seema*

○ Δυστυχώς όχι. Τίποτ' άλλο;
*dheesteeh**o**s **o**hee. t**ee**pot **a**lo*

\- Αυτά, ευχαριστώ.
*aft**a** efhareest**o***

○ Έντεκα ευρώ και πενήντα λεπτά.
e**ndeka evr**o** ke pen**ee**nda lept**a

Q They have stamps: true or false?

Buying Things

shops

baker's	ο φούρνος	*o f**oo**rnos*
butcher's	το κρεοπωλείο	*to kreopol**ee**o*
cake shop	το ζαχαροπλαστείο	*to zaharoplast**ee**o*
chemist's	το φαρμακείο	*to farmak**ee**o*
clothes shop	το κατάστημα ενδυμάτων	*to kat**a**steema endheem**a**ton*
dairy shop	το γαλακτοπωλείο	*to ghalaktopol**ee**o*
department store	το πολυκατάστημα	*to poleekat**a**steema*
fishmonger's	το ιχθυοπωλείο	*to eehtheeopol**ee**o*
greengrocer's	το μανάβικο	*to man**a**veeko*
grocer's	το παντοπωλείο	*to pandopol**ee**o*
jeweller's	το κοσμηματοπωλείο	*to kozmeematopol**ee**o*
kiosk (newsagent)	το περίπτερο	*to per**ee**ptero*
optician's	το κατάστημα οπτικών (οπτικά)	*to kat**a**steema opteek**o**n (opteek**a**)*
photographic shop	το φωτογραφείο	*to fotoghraf**ee**o*
supermarket	το σουπερμάρκετ	*to sooperm**a**rket*
travel agent's	το ταξιδιωτικό πρακτορείο	*to takseedheeoteek**o** praktor**ee**o*
shoe shop	το κατάστημα υποδημάτων/ υποδηματοπωλείο	*to kat**a**steema eepodheem**a**ton/ eepodheema-topol**ee**o*
shopping centre	εμπορικό κέντρο	*emboreek**o** k**e**ndro*

quantities

you may say ...

How much ... a kilo? is it are they	Πόσο ... το κιλό; κάνει κάνουν	*p**o**so ... to keel**o*** *k**a**nee* *k**a**noon*
A kilo of ... please. apples tomatoes cherries flour	Ένα κιλό ... παρακαλώ. μήλα ντομάτες κεράσια αλεύρι	***e**na keel**o** ... parakal**o*** *m**ee**la* *dom**a**tes* *ker**a**seea* *al**e**vree*

half a kilo	μισό κιλό	meeso keelo
quarter kilo	το τέταρτο	to tetarto
100 grammes of sweets	Εκατό γραμμάρια καραμέλες	ekato ghramareea karameles
a slice of ...	μία φετα ...	meea feta
three slices of ...	τρεις φέτες ...	trees fetes
Can I try ...	Μπορώ να δοκιμάσω ...	boro na dhokeemaso
some?	λίγο;	leegho
a piece?	ένα κομμάτι;	ena komatee
a bit more/less	λίγο ακόμα/πιο λίγο.	leegho akoma/peeo leegho
a litre/half a litre	ένα λίτρο/μισό λίτρο	ena leetro/meeso leetro
bottle	το μπουκάλι	to bookalee
jar	το βάζο	to vazo
packet	το πακέτο	to paketo
tin	η κονσέρβα	ee konserva
sachet	το σακουλάκι	to sakoolakee

you may hear ...

Πόσο/Πόσα θα θέλατε;	poso/posa tha thelate	How much/many would you like?
Φτάνει;	ftanee	Enough?

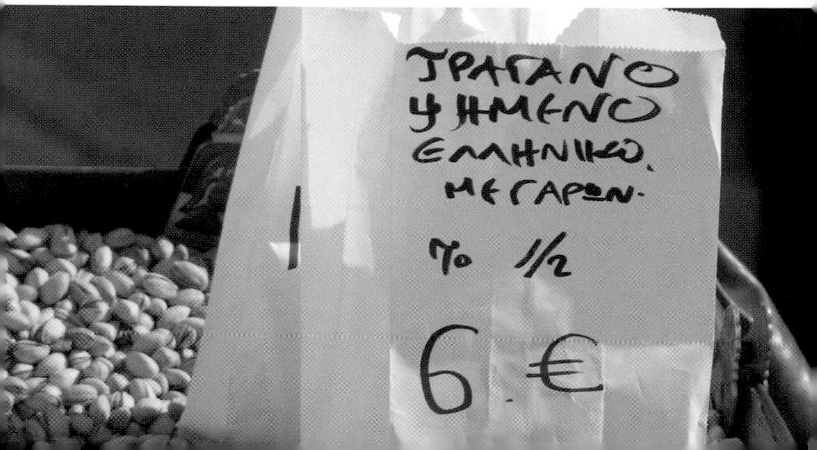

fruit & vegetables

apples	τα μήλα	*ta m**ee**la*
apricots	τα βερίκοκα	*ta ver**ee**koka*
asparagus	το σπαράγγι	*to spar**a**gee*
aubergine	η μελιτζάνα	*ee meleeds**a**na*
avocado	το αβοκάντο	*to avok**a**do*
bananas	οι μπανάνες	*ee ban**a**nes*
cabbage	το λάχανο	*to l**a**hano*
carrots	τα καρότα	*ta kar**o**ta*
cherries	τα κεράσια	*ta ker**a**seea*
courgette	το κολοκυθάκι	*to kolokeeth**a**kee*
cucumber	το αγγούρι	*to ang**oo**ree*
figs	τα σύκα	*ta s**ee**ka*
garlic	το σκόρδο	*to sk**o**rdho*
grapefruit	το γκρέιπ φρουτ	*to grape fruit*
grapes	το σταφύλι	*to staf**ee**lee*
kiwi fruit	το ακτινίδιο	*to akteen**ee**dheeo*
lemons	τα λεμόνια	*ta lem**o**neea*
lettuce	το μαρούλι	*to mar**oo**lee*
melon	το πεπόνι	*to pep**o**nee*
mushrooms	τα μανιτάρια	*ta maneet**a**reea*
onions	τα κρεμμύδια	*ta krem**ee**dheea*
oranges	τα πορτοκάλια	*ta portok**a**leea*
peaches	τα ροδάκινα	*ta rodh**a**keena*
pears	τα αχλάδια	*ta ahl**a**dheea*
peas	ο αρακάς	*o arak**a**s*
peppers	οι πιπεριές	*ee peeperee**e**s*
pineapple	ο ανανάς	*o anan**a**s*
pomegranates	τα ρόδια	*ta r**o**dheea*
potatoes	οι πατάτες	*ee pat**a**tes*
strawberries	οι φράουλες	*ee fr**a**ooles*
spinach	το σπανάκι	*to span**a**kee*
tomatoes	οι ντομάτες	*ee dom**a**tes*
watermelon	το καρπούζι	*to karp**oo**zee*

(For more food, see the Menu Reader, pp95-100)

check out 2

You are shopping in a fruit market in Athens.

- ❍ Να σας βοηθήσω;
  *na sas voeeth**ee**so*
- \- Ένα καρπούζι, δύο κιλά ντομάτες και τρία λεμόνια, παρακαλώ.
  e**na karp**oo**zee dh**ee**o keel**a** dom**a**tes ke tr**ee**a lem**o**nia parakal**o
- ❍ Ορίστε
  *or**ee**ste*
- \- Πόσο κάνουν όλα μαζί;
  *p**o**so k**a**noon **o**la maz**ee***
- ❍ Δώδεκα ευρώ και τριάντα λεπτά.
  *dh**o**dheka evr**o** ke tree**a**nda lept**a***
- \- Ευχαριστώ. Γεια σας.
  *efhareest**o**. ya sas*
- ❍ Γεια σας, ευχαριστώ.
  *ya sas efhareest**o***

Q How much did you pay in total?

fish & meat

beef	το βοδινό	*to vodheen**o***
chicken	το κοτόπουλο	*to kot**o**poolo*
cod	ο μπακαλιάρος	*o bakalee**a**ros*
ham	το ζαμπόν	*to zamb**o**n*
lamb	το αρνί/αρνάκι	*to arn**ee**/arn**a**kee*
pork	το χοιρινό	*to heereen**o***
sausage	το λουκάνικο	*to look**a**neeko*

groceries

bread	το ψωμί	*to psomee*
butter	το βούτυρο	*to vooteero*
cheese	το τυρί	*to teeree*
eggs	τα αβγά	*ta avgha*
honey	το μέλι	*to melee*
milk	το γάλα	*to ghala*
orange juice	ο χυμός πορτοκάλι	*o heemos potrokalee*
soap	το σαπούνι	*to sapoonee*
toilet roll	το χαρτί τουαλέτας	*to hartee tooaletas*
washing powder	το απορρυπαντικό	*to aporeepanteeko*
washing-up liquid	το υγρό για πιάτα	*to eeghro ya peeata*

(For toiletries, see p123)

check out 3

You are in a grocer's, buying food for a picnic.

- Μήπως έχετε ζαμπόν;
  meepos ehete zambon
- Ναι. Πόσο θέλετε;
  ne. poso thelete
- Ένα τέταρτο ζαμπόν και εκατό γραμμάρια τυρί.
  ena tetarto zambon ke ekato ghramareea teeree
- Τίποτ' άλλο;
  teepot alo
- Ναι, λίγη ταραμοσαλάτα.
  ne leeyee taramosalata
- Φτάνει;
  ftanee
- Ναι, ευχαριστώ. Αυτά.
  ne efhareesto. afta

Q You asked for a quarter of a kilo of cheese: true or false?

buying clothes

you may say ...

I'm just looking, thank you.	Απλά κοιτάω, ευχαριστώ.	*apla keetao efhareesto*
I'd like ... a shirt. a pair of trousers.	Θέλω ... ένα πουκάμισο. ένα παντελόνι.	*thelo* *ena pookameeso* *ena pandelonee*
I'm size 40.	Το νούμερό μου είναι σαράντα.	*to noomero mou eene saranda*
May I try ... on? it them	Μπορώ να ... δοκιμάσω; το τα	*boro na ... dhokee-maso* *to* *ta*
It's a bit ... big. small.	Είναι λίγο ... μεγάλο. μικρό.	*eene leegho* *meghalo* *meekro*
They're a bit ... big. small.	Είναι λίγο ... μεγάλα. μικρά.	*eene leegho* *meghala* *meekra*
Do you have anything ... smaller? cheaper?	Έχετε κάτι ... μικρότερο; φθηνότερο;	*ehete katee* *meekrotero* *ftheenotero*
Do you have the same in ... yellow? green? cotton? wool/100% wool?	Έχετε το ίδιο στο ... κίτρινο; πράσινο; βαμβακερό; μάλλινο/ολόμαλλο;	*ehete to eedeeo sto* *keetreeno* *praseeno* *vamvakero* *maleeno/olomalo*
I like it/them.	Μου αρέσει/αρέσουν.	*moo aresee/aresoon*
I don't like it/them.	Δεν μου αρέσει/ αρέσουν.	*dhen moo aresee/ aresoon*
I'll take it/them.	Θα το/τα πάρω.	*tha to/ta paro*
I'll think about it.	Θα το σκεφτώ.	*tha to skefto*

you may hear ...

Τι ... μέγεθος; νούμερο; χρώμα;	*tee* *m**e**yethos* *n**oo**mero* *hr**o**ma*	What ... size? (e.g. medium) size? (e.g. 40) colour?
Πώς σας φαίνεται/ φαίνονται;	*pos sas f**e**nete/ f**e**nonde*	How do you like it/them?
Είναι ... μεταξωτό. δερμάτινο. συνθετικό.	***ee**ne* *metaksot**o*** *dherm**a**teeno* *seentheteek**o***	It's ... silk. leather. synthetic.
Σας πάει!	*sas p**a**ee*	It suits you!
Σας πάνε!	*sas p**a**ne*	They suit you!

clothes & accessories

bag	η τσάντα	*ee ts**a**nda*
belt	η ζώνη	*ee z**o**nee*
coat	το παλτό	*to palt**o***
dress	το φόρεμα	*to f**o**rema*
handkerchief	το μαντήλι	*to mand**ee**lee*
hat	το καπέλο	*to kap**e**lo*
jacket	το σακάκι	*to sak**a**kee*
sandals	τα πέδιλα	*ta p**e**dheela*
scarf	το μαντήλι	*to mant**ee**lee*
shirt/blouse	το πουκάμισο	*to pook**a**meeso*
shoes	τα παπούτσια	*ta pap**oo**tseea*
shorts	το σορτς	*to s**o**rts*
skirt	η φούστα	*ee f**oo**sta*
socks	οι κάλτσες	*ee k**a**ltses*
suit	το κουστούμι	*to kost**oo**mee*
sunglasses	τα γυαλιά ηλίου	*ta yalee**a** eel**ee**oo*
sweater	το πουλόβερ	*to p**oo**lover*
swimming costume/ trunks	το μαγιό	*to may**o***
T-shirt	το φανελάκι	*to fanel**a**kee*
underwear	τα εσώρουχα	*ta es**o**rooha*

department store

you may say ...

Where is the ... department?	Πού είναι το τμήμα με ...	*poo **ee**ne to tm**ee**ma me*
ladies'	τα γυναικεία;	*ta gheenek**ee**a*
men's	τα ανδρικά;	*ta andhreek**a***
kids'	τα παιδικά;	*ta pedheek**a***
toy	τα παιχνίδια;	*ta pehn**ee**dheea*
cosmetics	τα καλλυντικά;	*ta kaleendeek**a***
Where can I find ...	Πού είναι ...	*poo **ee**ne*
shoes?	τα παπούτσια;	*ta pap**oo**tseea*
underwear?	τα εσώρουχα;	*ta es**o**rooha*
Is there a lift?	Υπάρχει ασανσέρ;	*eep**a**rhee asans**e**r*
Where are the checkouts?	Πού είναι το ταμείο;	*poo **ee**ne to tam**ee**o*

you may hear ...

Στο ...	*sto*	On the ...
ισόγειο.	*ees**o**gheeo*	ground floor.
δεύτερο όροφο.	*d**e**ftero **o**rofo*	second floor.
Στον πρώτο όροφο.	*ston pr**o**to **o**rofo*	On the first floor.
Στο υπόγειο.	*sto eep**o**gheeo*	In the basement.

check out 3

You would like to buy a pair of trousers.

- Θέλω ένα μαύρο παντελόνι.
  thelo ena mavro pandelonee
- Τι νούμερο;
  tee noomero
- Σαράντα τέσσερα.
  saranda tesera
- Έχουμε μόνο μπλε και καφέ.
  ehoome mono ble ke kafe
- Μπορώ να δοκιμάσω το καφέ;
  boro na dhokeemaso to kafe

Q Do they have black trousers?

buying stamps

you may say ...

How much is a stamp for ...	Πόσο κάνει ένα γραμματόσημο για ...	*poso kanee ena ghramatoseemo ya*
Great Britain?	την Μεγάλη Βρετανία;	*teen meghalee vretaneea*
the United States?	την Αμερική;	*teen amereekee*
for a ...	για ...	*ya*
letter	γράμμα	*ghrama*
postcard	κάρτα	*karta*
Two 50 cent stamps, please.	Δύο γραμματόσημα των πενήντα λεπτών, παρακαλώ.	*dheeo ghramatoseema ton peneenda lepton parakalo*
I'd like to send this to Australia.	Θέλω να στείλω αυτό στην Αυστραλία.	*thelo na steelo afto steen afstraleea*

photography

you may say ...

I'd like ...	Θέλω ...	*th**e**lo*
batteries.	μπαταρίες.	*batar**ee**es*
a memory card.	μία κάρτα μνήμης.	*m**ee**a k**a**rta mn**ee**mees*
a disposable camera.	μία μηχανή μιας χρήσεως.	*m**ee**a meehan**ee** mee**a**s hr**ee**seos*
a colour/black and white film.	ένα έγχρωμο/ ασπρόμαυρο φιλμ.	***e**na **e**nhromo/ aspr**o**mavro feelm*
Can you develop this?	Μπορείτε να το εμφανίσετε;	*bor**ee**te na to emfan**ee**sete*
Do you print digital photos?	Εκτυπώνετε ψηφιακές φωτογραφίες;	*ekteep**o**nete pseefeeak**e**s fotoghraf**ee**es*
When will it/they be ready?	Πότε θα είναι έτοιμο/ έτοιμες;	*p**o**te tha **ee**ne **e**teemo/**e**teemes*
I have a digital camera.	Έχω ψηφιακή μηχανή.	***e**ho pseefeeak**ee** meehan**ee***

you may hear ...

σήμερα	*s**ee**mera*	today
αύριο	***a**vreeo*	tomorrow
σε ...	*se*	in ...
μία ώρα	*m**ee**a **o**ra*	one hour
τρεις ώρες	*trees **o**res*	three hours
Τι μέγεθος;	*tee m**e**yethos*	What size?
ματ	*mat*	matt
γυαλιστερές	*yaleester**e**s*	glossy

sound check

The letters **ΜΠ**, **μπ** combine to make a 'b' sound, as in 'bed':

μπεζ *bez* μπισκότο *beesk**o**to*

λάμπα *l**a**mba*

try it out

mind the gap

Fill in the missing vowels to make words for food, e.g. ν_ρ_ = νερό.

1 τ_ρ_
2 γ_ _ _ _ ρτ _
3 ζ_μπ_ν
4 ψ_μ_
5 π_π_ν_
6 ντ_μ_τ_

money talk

Add up what the items below cost.

a loaf of bread	– εξήντα πέντε λεπτά	....
three stamps to England	– ένα ευρώ και ενενήντα πέντε λεπτά	....
a magazine	– τρία ευρώ	....
	total: .... ευρώ	

as if you were there

You're doing your shopping in a small grocer's. Follow the prompts to play your part.

(Ask for 250 grammes of feta)
(Then ask for two hundred grammes of ham and some taramosalata)
Φτάνει η ταραμοσαλάτα;
(Ask for a little bit more)
Τίποτ' άλλο;
(Ask for three lemons and a bar of chocolate. Then say, that's all)
Οχτώ ευρώ, παρακαλώ.
(Say there you are)
Ευχαριστώ, τα ρέστα σας.
(Say you're welcome, then goodbye)

linkup

key phrases

Έχετε ντομάτες; *ehete domates*	**Do you have** any tomatoes?
Θέλω δύο κιλά. *thelo dheeo keela*	**I want** two kilos.
Μ' αρέσει το κρασί. *maresee to krasee*	**I like** wine.
Μ' αρέσουν τα μπισκότα. *maresoon ta beeskota*	**I like** biscuits.
Πόσο κάνει η φούστα; *poso kanee ee foosta*	**How much is** the skirt?
Πόσο κάνουν τα παπούτσια; *poso kanoon ta papootseea*	**How much are** the shoes?

comparing things

When out shopping, if you want to ask for something smaller or cheaper, add **πιο** *peeo* before the relevant adjective:

Έχετε **πιο μικρή** φούστα; Do you have a **smaller** skirt?
ehete peeo meekree foosta
(literally, Do you have a more small skirt?)

Θέλω κάτι **πιο φτηνό**. I want something **cheaper.**
thelo katee peeo fteeno
(literally, I want something more cheap)

This also works for bigger:
Έχετε **πιο μεγάλο** νούμερο; Do you have a **bigger** size?
ehete peeo meghalo noomero
(literally, Do you have a more big size?)

how to say you like something

For likes and dislikes, Greek uses the idea of 'pleasing':
Μ' αρέσει η φούστα. I like the skirt.
maresee ee foosta
(literally, The skirt is pleasing to me)

So for dislikes you can say:
Δεν μ' αρέσει το κρασί. I don't like wine.
dhen maresee to krasee

And when what you like is plural, you say:
Μ' αρέσουν τα βερίκοκα. I like apricots.
maresoon ta vereekoka

Δεν μ' αρέσουν τα ροδάκινα. I don't like peaches.
dhen maresoon ta rodhakeena

Note that when saying what you like or don't like in Greek, you need to use the word for 'the'.

For more on expressing likes and dislikes, and when to use 'the' in Greek, see the Language Builder p139 and p132.

Café **Life**

where to go

Cafés are what Greek life is all about; sipping a drink and watching the world go by. They also serve food and dessert and are open all day, getting busy from after siesta time until the small hours. Many Greeks have a pastry with their afternoon coffee.

Καφενείο *kafeneeo* These traditional coffee shops cater for the older-generation local men. Larger ones offer tea and drinks (alcoholic and soft). Few serve food, but they are the perfect place for a drink stop. Tourists are usually welcomed.

Ζαχαροπλαστείο *zaharoplasteeo* (patisserie or sweet shop) These are your best bet for a non-tourist breakfast or homemade cake. Most are takeaway only.

Φούρνος *foornos* (baker's) These sell – along with bread – milk, yoghurt, drinks, ice cream, sweets and biscuits and tasty snacks such as τυρόπιτες *teeropeetes* (cheese pies).

Γαλακτοπωλείο *galaktopoleeo* These dairy shops/alternative cafés sell yoghurt, rice pudding and ice cream.

Ουζερί / Μεζεδοπωλείο *ouzeree/mezedhopoleeo* These provide μεζέδες *mezedhes* (snacks) with ouzo, or beer if you prefer. Try ordering a ποικιλία *peekeeleea* which is a selection of sausage, cheese and salad.

Μπυραρία *beerareea* are beer houses also serving snacks such as toasted sandwiches. Some of the more up-market establishments have beer gardens and offer a variety of imported beers.

what to drink

Ouzo This aniseed-flavoured national speciality is sometimes diluted with water, and should be accompanied by a small plate of μεζέ *meze* such as octopus or cheese. It is made from the pulp remaining at the end of the wine-making process.

Tsipouro/Raki A fierce version of ouzo, similar to grappa.

Retsina A pine-resinated wine which people associate with 'the flavour of Greece', though it can be an acquired taste.

Barrelled wine Known as χύμα *heema* or βαρελίσιο *vareleeseeo*. This can be resinated or non-resinated, white or red and is one of the cheapest and best drinks around. It is served by the kilo – a large jug – or half-kilo.

Bottled wines Greek wines are little known outside the country but there is a large variety to suit all palates. Brands commonly found in restaurants include Tsantali (including Agioritiko and Makedonikos), Hatzimichali and Domaine Carras. If you want to sample a local wine, ask for ντόπιο κρασί *dopeeo krasee*.

Metaxa The national brandy is a perfect nightcap, available as a three-, five- or seven-star drink. The three-star is on the rough side and nowadays more difficult to find, the seven-star is smooth.

Greek coffee This is dark and thick, made in a tiny pot and served in a small cup. Order it σκέτο *sketo* (without sugar), μέτριο *metreeo* (medium sweet) or γλυκό *gleeko* (sweet). Sip it when the grounds have settled.

Frappé (iced coffee) The best way to drink coffee in the Greek summer. For a luxury version try asking for φραπέ με παγωτό *frappe me paghoto* (with a scoop of vanilla ice cream).

Fruit liqueurs Most families make their own brandy-based fruit liqueurs, and most regions specialise in one type. Look for sour cherry.

phrasemaker

ordering

you may say ...

Do you have any ...	Έχετε ...	ehete
sandwiches?	σάντουιτς;	sandooeets
grapefruit juice?	χυμό γκρέιπ φρουτ;	heemo greeep froot
mineral water?	μεταλλικό νερό;	metaleeko nero
What ... do you have?	Τι ... έχετε;	tee ... ehete
snacks	πρόχειρο φαγητό	proheero fayeeto
cakes	γλυκά	ghleeka
ice creams	παγωτά	paghota
What ... do you have?	Τι ... έχετε;	tee ... ehete
soft drinks	αναψυκτικά	anapseekteeka
(fruit) juices	χυμούς	heemoos
I'd like ...	Θα ήθελα ...	tha eethela
an iced coffee.	ένα φραπέ.	ena frappe
a cup of tea.	ένα τσάι.	ena tsaee
(I'll have) ... please.	... παρακαλώ.	... parakalo
a cheese sandwich	Ένα σάντουιτς με τυρί	ena sandooeets me teeree
a pancake	Μία κρέπα	meea krepa
a white coffee	Ένα καφέ με γάλα	ena kafe me ghala
an orange juice	Ένα χυμό πορτοκάλι	ena heemo portokalee
(I'll have) a ... ice cream, please.	Παγωτό ... παρακαλώ.	paghoto ... parakalo
strawberry	φράουλα	fraoola
lemon	λεμόνι	lemonee
this one/that one	αυτό/εκείνο	afto/ekeeno

you may hear…

Ορίστε. Παρακαλώ;	*oreeste parakalo*	What would you like?
Τι θα θέλατε;	*tee tha thelate*	What would you like?
Συγνώμη, μας τελείωσε.	*seeghnomee mas teleeose*	I'm sorry, we've run out.
Με ...	*me*	With ...
πάγο;	*pagho*	ice?
λεμόνι;	*lemonee*	lemon?
με ανθρακικό/ χωρίς ανθρακικό	*me anthrakeeko/ horees anthrakeeko*	fizzy/still
Ποιο;	*peeo*	Which one?
Πληρώστε στο ταμείο, παρακαλώ.	*pleeroste sto tameeo parakalo*	Please pay at the till.
Είναι σελφ-σέρβις.	*eene self servees*	It's self-service.
Τι παγωτό θέλετε;	*tee paghoto thelete*	Which (flavour) ice cream?
Έχουμε ...	*ehoome*	We have ...
κεράσι.	*kerasee*	cherry.
σοκολάτα.	*sokolata*	chocolate.
φιστίκι.	*feesteekee*	pistachio.
φράουλα.	*fraoola*	strawberry.
κρέμα.	*krema*	vanilla.
Τίποτ' άλλο;	*teepot alo*	Anything else?

snacks

cheese pie	η τυρόπιτα	*ee teeropeeta*
spinach pie	η σπανακόπιτα	*ee spanakopeeta*
doner kebab	ο γύρος	*o yeeros*
hot/cold sandwich	Το ζεστό/κρύο σάντουιτς	*to zesto/kreeo sandooeets*
with ...	με ...	*me*
ham	ζαμπόν	*zambon*
cheese	τυρί	*teeree*
sausage	λουκάνικο	*lookaneeko*
omelette	η ομελέτα	*ee omeleta*
spaghetti	η μακαρονάδα	*ee makaronadha*
toast	η φρυγανιά	*ee freeghaneea*

desserts & cakes

baklava (layers of pastry, nuts, honey)	ο μπακλαβάς	*o baklav**a**s*
biscuit	το μπισκότο	*to beesk**o**to*
cake	η τούρτα	*ee t**oo**rta*
slice of cake	η πάστα	*ee p**a**sta*
almond cake	η πάστα αμυγδάλου	*ee p**a**sta ameeghdh**a**loo*
chocolate/orange cake	το κέικ πορτοκάλι/ σοκολάτα	*to k**e**eek portok**a**lee/ sokol**a**ta*
cakes in syrup	τα γλυκά ταψιού	*ta ghleek**a** tapsee**oo***
walnut cake	η καρυδόπιτα	*ee kareedh**o**peeta*
chocolate (gateaux)	η σοκολατίνα	*ee sokolat**ee**na*
cookie	το κουλουράκι	*to koulour**a**kee*
custard pie	το γαλακτομπούρεκο	*to ghalaktob**oo**reko*
honey fritters with cinnamon	λουκουμάδες	*lookoom**a**dhes*
fruit salad	η φρουτοσαλάτα	*ee frootosal**a**ta*
nougat	η νουγκατίνα	*ee noogat**ee**na*
pancake	η κρέπα	*ee kr**e**pa*
profiterole	το προφιτερόλ	*to profeeter**o**l*
waffle	η βάφλα	*ee v**a**fla*

check out 1

You've stopped for a snack while out shopping.

- Ένα σάντουιτς με ζαμπόν και τυρί, παρακαλώ.
  ena sandooeets me zambon ke teeree parakalo
- Μάλιστα. Πληρώστε στο ταμείο παρακαλώ.
  maleesta. pleeroste sto tameeo parakalo

Q What did you order?

hot drinks

cappuccino	ο καπουτσίνο	*o kapootseeno*
hot/cold chocolate	η ζεστή/κρύα σοκολάτα	*ee zestee/kreea sokolata*
coffee	ο καφές	*o kafes*
coffee (hot)	ο νες (ζεστός)	*o nes (zestos)*
filter coffee	ο καφές φίλτρου	*o kafes feeltroo*
white coffee	ο καφές με γάλα	*o kafes me ghala*
decaffeinated	ο ντεκαφεϊνέ	*o dekafee-ene*
espresso	ο εσπρέσο	*o espreso*
Greek coffee	ο ελληνικός καφές	*o eleeneekos kafes*
tea	το τσάι	*to tsaee*
camomile tea	το χαμομήλι	*to hamomeelee*
mint tea	το τσάι μέντα	*to tsaee menda*
sweet/medium sweet	γλυκός/μέτριος	*ghleekos/metreeos*
with ... cream milk whipped cream	με ... κρέμα γάλα σαντιγί	*me* *krema* *ghala* *sandeeyee*
without sugar	σκέτος/χωρίς ζάχαρη	*sketos/horees zaharee*

alcoholic drinks

aperitif	το απεριτίφ	*to apereeteef*
beer, lager	η μπύρα	*ee beera*
brandy	το μπράντι	*to brandee*
draught beer	η βαρελίσια μπύρα	*ee vareleeseea beera*
gin	το τζιν	*to dseen*
ouzo	το ούζο	*to oozo*
red/rosé/white wine	το κρασί κόκκινο/ ροζέ/άσπρο	*to krasee kokeeno/ roze/aspro*
retsina	η ρετσίνα	*ee retseena*
rum	το ρούμι	*to roomee*
sherry	το σέρρυ	*to seree*
sour cherry liqueur	το λικέρ βύσσινο	*to leeker veeseeno*
sweet/dry	γλυκό/ξηρό	*ghleeko/kseero*
whisky	το ουίσκι	*to ooeeskee*

check out 2

You are ordering drinks for yourself and some friends in a café.

❍ Ορίστε. Παρακαλώ.
oreeste parakalo

- Δύο μπουκάλια μπύρα, παρακαλώ.
dheeo bookaleea beera parakalo

❍ Τίποτ' άλλο;
teepot alo

- Ένα ούζο με πάγο και έναν ελληνικό καφέ.
ena oozo me pagho ke enan eleeneeko kafe

❍ Δώδεκα ευρώ παρακαλώ.
dhodheka evro parakalo

- Ορίστε. Ευχαριστώ.
oreeste. efhareesto

Q How much did you pay?

soft drinks

coke	η κόκα κόλα	*ee k**o**ka k**o**la*
fruit juices	οι χυμοί φρούτων	*ee heem**ee** fr**oo**ton*
iced coffee	ο φραπέ	*o frap**e***
iced tea	το παγωμένο τσάι	*to paghom**e**no ts**a**ee*
lemonade	η λεμονάδα	*ee lemon**a**dha*
milkshake	το μιλκ σέικ	*to meelk s**e**eek*
mineral water	το μεταλλικό νερό	*to metaleek**o** ner**o***
mixed fruit juice	ο ανάμικτος χυμός	*o an**a**meektoos heem**o**s*
orangeade	η πορτοκαλάδα	*ee portokal**a**dha*
orange/lemon/peach juice	ο χυμός πορτοκάλι/ λεμόνι/ροδάκινο	*o heem**o**s portok**a**lee/ lem**o**nee/rodh**a**k**ee**no*
sherbet (crushed ice drink)	η γρανίτα	*ee ghran**ee**ta*
soda/tonic water	η σόδα/το τόνικ	*ee s**o**dha/to t**o**neek*

check out 3

You are ordering ice cream.

- ❍ Τι παγωτά έχετε;
  *tee paghot**a** **e**hete*
- \- Σοκολάτα, φράουλα, κρέμα.
  *sokol**a**ta fr**a**oola kr**e**ma*
- ❍ Έχετε φιστίκι;
  ***e**hete feest**ee**kee*
- \- Μας τελείωσε.
  *mas tel**ee**ose*
- ❍ Ένα σοκολάτα παρακαλώ.
  e**na sokol**a**ta parakal**o
- \- Μάλιστα.
  *m**a**leesta*

Q Do they have any pistachio ice cream?
You order vanilla ice cream: true or false?

sound check

It is important to notice the use of accents in Greek words, as they tell you which syllable to stress. For example:

παρακαλώ *parakal**o*** (the stress falls on ***lo*** at the end)
μπύρα *b**ee**ra* (the stress falls on the first syllable **bee**)
σοκολάτα *soko**la**ta* (the stress falls on the third syllable ***la***)

Practise on these words:

λεμονάδα *lemon**a**dha*
σόδα *s**o**dha*
τυρί *teer**ee***
κρασί *kras**ee***

try it out

order, order

Put the following drinks into the correct category:
a) cold drinks, b) hot drinks, c) alcoholic drinks.

1 φραπέ
2 ούζο
3 κρασί κόκκινο
4 ροφήματα
5 γρανίτα
6 καφές
7 τσάι
8 χυμός πορτοκάλι
9 τζιν
10 καπουτσίνο
11 μπύρα

as if you were there

You and your friend have found a nice café. Follow the prompts to play your part.

(Ask what kind of cakes they have)
Σοκολατίνα, νουγκατίνα, αμυγδάλου.
(Ask if they have any sherbet)
Μας τελείωσε.
(Order a chocolate cake and an orangeade)
Μάλιστα.

linkup

Έχετε παγωτό; *ehete paghoto*	**Do you have** any ice cream?
Τι μπύρα **έχετε**; *tee beera ehete*	**What** beer **do you have**?
Ένα τσάι **παρακαλώ**. *ena tsaee parakalo*	A/One tea, **please**.
Θα ήθελα ένα τοστ με τυρί και ζαμπόν. *tha eethela ena tost me teeree ke zambon*	**I'd like** a cheese and ham toasted sandwich.

asking for something

The easiest way is simply to state what you want:
Μία πορτοκαλάδα, παρακαλώ. An orangeade, please.
meea portokaladha parakalo
Ένα παγωτό, παρακαλώ. An ice cream, please.
ena paghoto parakalo
You can add 'please', though it's less common than in English.

Some more possibilities are:
Θα ήθελα ένα φραπέ. I'd like a frappé.
tha eethela ena frappe
Θα πάρω ένα τοστ. I'll have a toasted sandwich.
tha paro ena tost
or if you're ordering for yourself and other people:
Θα πάρουμε μία πίτσα. We'll have a pizza.
tha paroome meea peetsa
Μου δίνετε μία απόδειξη; May I have (Could you give me) a receipt? *moo dheenete meea apodheeksee*

This is said as a question, with rising intonation.

Eating **Out**

For the Greeks, eating out is a popular and inexpensive social event. Children and large groups are always welcome. Lunch may be eaten from around 12.30 to as late as 5pm. Restaurants will serve dinner from 7pm but most locals won't eat until 9pm, often lingering over this meal until beyond midnight. All cafés and restaurants have non-smoking areas, but these tend to be small as a majority of Greeks are heavy smokers.

where to eat

Εστιατόριο *esteeat**o**reeo*
These restaurants serve good-quality food in an informal atmosphere. In some, you may be invited into the kitchen to choose your dish. Restaurants tend not to vary widely in terms of quality, but if you want to dine in style try one of the increasing number of up-market restaurants serving Aegean nouvelle cuisine.

Ταβέρνα *tav**e**rna* A meal in a taverna can be a lively, atmospheric affair, with Greek musicians playing and singing, and wine flowing from the barrel. A tray of appetisers and side dishes may be brought for you to select from. Look out also for **της ώρας** *tees **o**ras*, meaning meat which is grilled or fried on the spot (as opposed to cooked in advance, common practice in restaurants). Tavernas tend to be open in the evenings only, till 1 or 2am.

Μεζεδοπωλείο/Ουζερί *mezedopol**ee**o/ouzer**ee*** A good place for a lighter meal and a drink. Almost indistinguishable from tavernas.

Ψησταριά *pseestaree**a*** (grill house) These can be identified by the smell of sizzling meat. They are especially popular in inland market and mountain towns and serve meat dishes and simple salads.

Ψαροταβέρνα *psarotav**e**rna* A taverna specialising in fish and seafood dishes, these also usually open for lunch as well as dinner. Fish is charged by weight.

what to eat

Greek meals can last a long time, and revolve around separate dishes rather than courses. A typical meal consists of a selection of **μεζέδες** *mezedhes*, followed by a meat or fish dish (usually accompanied by just a slice of lemon and a few chips). If you don't want all your dishes to arrive at once, order them at different times.

A menu may be divided into **ορεκτικά** *orekteeka* (starters), **εντράδες** *entrades* (main dishes) and **γλυκά** *ghleeka* (dessert). In Greece, desserts tend to be eaten as a snack with afternoon coffee – see Café Life – so expect sweet options to be limited to fruit, yoghurt or ice cream.

For the best food, it is always a good idea to see where the locals eat and what they order. Most dishes are cooked in a lot of olive oil; you may wish to ask for salads without it if you feel things are too oily. Also, do not be surprised if your food is luke-warm, as many dishes are cooked in the morning and allowed to cool; hot food is considered bad for the digestion.

Here is a selection of some well-known dishes to try. Bear in mind that Greek cuisine relies on seasonal produce and some of these will only be available for part of the year.

Σουβλάκι *souvlakee* Tender meat (usually pork) served on a skewer with pitta bread.

Μουσακάς *mousakas* Layers of aubergines, potatoes, mince and béchamel sauce.

Παπουτσάκια *papootsakeea* (literally 'small shoes') Aubergines stuffed with mince and topped with béchamel.

Ντολμάδες *dolmadhes* Rice with dill or mint wrapped in vine leaves, sometimes with mince. It may be served with **αυγολέμονο** *avgholemono* sauce (egg and lemon).

Στιφάδο *steefado* A traditional beef or game casserole, with baby onions in a rich sauce.

Μπριάμ *breeam* Vegetarian stew including courgettes, aubergines, tomatoes and sometimes peppers.

Γεμιστά *yemeesta* Peppers and tomatoes stuffed with delicately flavoured rice.

Μπακαλιάρος σκορδαλιά *bakaleearos skordhaleea* Cod cooked in batter and served with an often wickedly strong garlic potato mash.

Χωριάτικη σαλάτα *horeeateekee salata* Greek 'village' salad, containing onions, tomatoes, cucumber, green peppers and feta. When tomatoes are out of season, finely chopped lettuce salad is more common.

regional specialities

Attiki, around Athens Seafood fans may want to sample πιλάφι με θαλασσινά *peelafee me thalaseena* (seafood risotto) or αχινοί γεμιστοί *aheenee yemeestee* (stuffed sea urchins). Also popular: φυστίκια Αιγίνης *feesteekeea eyeenees* (pistachio nuts from Aegina).

The Cyclades Main dishes to try include γούνα *ghoona* (sun-dried, grilled mackerel); κολοκυθολούλουδα τηγανητά *kolokeetholooloodha teeghaneeta* (fried courgette flowers), κακαβιά *kakaveea* (fish soup) and κοπανιστή *kopaneestee* (a strong cheese salad). For those with a sweet tooth there are αμυγδαλωτά *ameeghdhalota* (almond sweets) and λουκούμια *lookoomeea* (Turkish Delight from Syros). To drink, try Κίτρο *keetro* (a sweet citrus liqueur from Naxos).

The Dodecanese Specialities include: ζυμαρικά με γιαούρτι *zeemareeka me yaoortee* (pasta with yoghurt and onion); κοριαντολίνο *koreeandoleeno* (a fruit liqueur from Rhodes) and μαρίδα πικάντικη *mareeda peekandeekee* (spicy whitebait).

Crete Worth a try are: boiled goat; στάκα *staka* (fried cheese); καλτσούνια *kaltsooneea* (sweet cheese pies); σαλιγκάρια στυφάδο *saleegareea steefadho* (snail stew).

The Peloponnese Look out for Μαυροδάφνη *mavrodhafnee* (a fortified red wine); Achaia Clauss wine (wine from Patras); γουρουνόπουλο *ghooroonopoolo* (spit-roast pork traditionally cooked when there is local celebration or festival) and παστέλι *pastelee* (sesame sweets).

Ionian islands Some specialities from this region are Ρομπόλα *robola* (red wine from Kefalonia); γραβιέρα *graveeera* (a Gruyere-type cheese); μπουρδέτο *boordheto* (rock fish with tomato and onion sauce); μαντολάτο *mandolato* (nougat from Zakinthos).

Northern and central mainland Greece Look out for φασολάδα *fasoladha* (bean soup); σπετζοφάι *spetzofaee* (spicy pork sausages with green peppers); πέστροφα *pestrofa* (trout); μύδια σαγανάκι *meedheea saghanakee* (fried mussels) and χαλβά *halva* (sweet pastry). Dessert or snack options include κουραμπιέδες *koorabeeedhes* (an almond biscuit-like sweet); τυρόψωμο *teeropsomo* (cheese bread) and μπουγάτσα *booghatsa* (cream pies).

Sporades Try γαρίδες σαγανάκι *ghareedhes saghanakee* (prawns baked with cheese and tomatoes); lobsters and seafood, and prunes from Skopelos.

North east Aegean λάχανο με κιμά *lahano me keema* (cabbage with mince), μαστίχα *masteeha* (a sweet aperitif from Hios); φιλιανοί ντολμάδες *feeleeanee dolmadhes* (minced meat rolled in onion skins); anchovies and ouzo from Lesvos.

phrasemaker

finding somewhere to eat

you may say ...

Is there a good restaurant near here?	Υπάρχει κανένα καλό εστιατόριο εδώ κοντά;	*eeparhee kanena kalo esteeatoreeo edho konda*
I'd like to book a table for ...	Θα ήθελα να κλείσω ένα τραπέζι για ...	*tha eethela na kleeso ena trapezee ya*
tomorrow night.	αύριο το βράδυ.	*avreeo to vradhee*
this evening at 8.30pm.	σήμερα το βράδυ στις οχτώ και μισή.	*seemera to vradhee stees ohto ke meesee*
four people.	τέσσερα άτομα.	*tesera atoma*

arriving

you may say ...

A table for two/four.	Ένα τραπέζι για δύο/ τέσσερεις.	*ena trapezee ya dheeo/teserees*
We have a reservation for ...	Έχουμε κλείσει για ...	*ehoome kleesee ya*
We haven't booked.	Δεν έχουμε κλείσει τραπέζι.	*dhen ehoome kleesee trapezee*
Is this table free?	Είναι ελεύθερο αυτό το τραπέζι;	*eene elefthero afto to trapezee*
Excuse me, is it self-service?	Συγνώμη, είναι σελφ-σέρβις;	*seeghnomee eene self servees*

you may hear ...

Ένα λεπτό, παρακαλώ.	*ena lepto parakalo*	One moment, please.
Λυπάμαι είμαστε γεμάτοι.	*leepame eemaste yematee*	Sorry, we're full.
Θέλετε να περιμένετε;	*thelete na pereemenete*	Would you like to wait?
Καπνίζοντες ή μη καπνίζοντες;	*kapneezondes ee mee kapneezondes*	Smoking or non-smoking?

Eating **Out**

check out 1

You ask for a table at a restaurant.

○ Καλησπέρα. Ένα τραπέζι για τέσσερα άτομα παρακαλώ.
kaleespera. ena trapezee ya tesera atoma parakalo

- Λυπάμαι είμαστε γεμάτοι. Θέλετε να περιμένετε;
leepame eemaste yematee. thelete na pereemenete

Q How many people are eating?
They have a free table: true or false?

asking about the menu

you may say ...

The menu/wine list, please.	Τον κατάλογο/ κατάλογο κρασιών, παρακαλώ.	*ton kat**a**logho/ kat**a**logho kraseе**o**n parakal**o***
What is ...?	Τι είναι ...;	*tee **ee**ne*
What do you recommend?	Τι συστήνετε (προτείνετε);	*tee seest**ee**nete (prot**ee**nete)*
What's the local speciality?	Ποια είναι η τοπική σπεσιαλιτέ;	*pee**a** **ee**ne ee topeek**ee** speseealeet**e***
Have you got ...?	Έχετε ...;	***e**hete*
I'm allergic ...	Είμαι αλλεργικός/ αλλεργική ...	***ee**me aleryeek**o**s/ aleryeek**ee***
to dairy.	στα γαλακτοκομικά.	*sta ghalaktokomeek**a***
to wheat.	στα προϊόντα σίτου.	*sta proee**o**nda s**ee**too*
I'm ...	Είμαι ...	***ee**me*
vegetarian.	χορτοφάγος.	*hortof**a**ghos*
vegan.	αυστηρά χορτοφάγος.	*afsteer**a** hortof**a**ghos*
diabetic.	διαβητικός/ διαβητική.	*dheeaveeteek**o**s/ dheeaveeteek**ee***
Does it contain ...	Περιέχει ...	*perее**e**hee*
nuts?	ξηρούς καρπούς;	*kseer**oo**s karp**oo**s*

you may hear ...

Σήμερα έχουμε ...	*s**ee**mera **e**hoome*	Today we have ...
Είναι ...	***ee**ne*	It's ...
κρέας.	*kr**e**as*	meat.
ψάρι.	*ps**a**ree*	fish.
λαχανικό.	*lahaneek**o***	a vegetable.
σάλτσα.	*s**a**ltsa*	a sauce.
Συγνώμη, δεν έχουμε ...	*seeghn**o**mee dhen **e**hoome*	Sorry, we don't have any ...

ordering

you may say ...

We are ready to order.	Είμαστε έτοιμοι να παραγγείλουμε.	***ee**maste **e**teemee na parang**ee**loome*
I'll have ...	Θα πάρω ...	*tha p**a**ro*
Will you bring me ... please? a chop a salad a portion of chips	(Μου φέρνετε) ... παρακαλώ; μία μπριζόλα μία σαλάτα μία μερίδα πατάτες τηγανητές	*(moo f**e**rnete) parakal**o*** *m**ee**a breez**o**la* *m**ee**a sal**a**ta* *m**ee**a mer**ee**dha pat**a**tes teeghaneet**e**s*
as a ... starter main course dessert	για ... πρώτο πιάτο κύριο πιάτο επιδόρπιο	*ya* *pr**o**to pee**a**to* *k**ee**reeo pee**a**to* *epeedh**o**rpeeo*
Does it come with vegetables?	Σερβίρεται με λαχανικά;	*serv**ee**rete me lahaneek**a***
No dessert, thank you.	Όχι επιδόρπιο, ευχαριστώ.	***o**hee epeedh**o**rpeeo efhareest**o***
rare	σενιάν	*seneea**n***
medium	μέτριο	*m**e**treeo*
well done	καλοψημένο	*kalopseem**e**no*
I'll have the same as him/her/them.	Θα πάρω το ίδιο με αυτόν/αυτήν/αυτούς.	*tha p**a**ro to **ee**dheeo me aft**o**n/aft**ee**/aft**oo**s*

you may hear ...

Τι θα πάρετε;	*tee tha p**a**rete*	What would you like?
Είστε έτοιμοι να παραγγείλετε;	***ee**ste **e**teemee na parag**ee**lete*	Are you ready to order?
Πώς θέλετε να το ψήσουμε;	*pos th**e**lete na to ps**ee**soome*	How would you like it done?
Θέλετε επιδόρπιο;	*th**e**lete epeedh**o**rpeeo*	Would you like a dessert?
Τι θα πιείτε;	*tee tha pee**ee**te*	To drink?
Καλή όρεξη!	*kal**ee** **o**reksee*	Enjoy your meal!

check out 2

You are eating out in a restaurant.

- ❍ Παρακαλώ;
  *parakal**o***
- \- Έχετε μουσακά;
  e**hete moosak**a
- ❍ Συγνώμη, δεν έχουμε. Έχουμε παπουτσάκια.
  *seeghn**o**mee dhen **e**hoome. **e**hoome papoots**a**keea*
- \- Τι είναι αυτό;
  *tee **ee**ne aft**o***
- ❍ Μελιτζάνες γεμιστές με κιμά.
  *meleeds**a**nes yemeest**e**s me keem**a***
- \- Ωραία. Παπουτσάκια, παρακαλώ.
  *or**e**a. papoots**a**keea parakal**o***

(Ωραία = fine)

Q Do they have moussaka?
What is 'παπουτσάκια'?

during the meal

you may say …

Excuse me! Waiter!	Συγνώμη! Παρακαλώ!	*seeghn**o**mee parakal**o***
I didn't order ...	Δεν παρήγγειλα ...	*dhen par**ee**ngeela*
Another (bottle of) ...	Ακόμα (ένα μπουκάλι) ...	*ak**o**ma (**e**na book**a**lee)*
More bread, please.	Ψωμί, παρακαλώ.	*psom**ee** parakal**o***
It's ... delicious. very good. cold. underdone.	Είναι ... νοστιμότατο. πολύ καλό. κρύο. άψητο.	***ee**ne* *nosteem**o**tato* *pole**e** kal**o*** *kr**ee**o* ***a**pseeto*
The glass is dirty.	Το ποτήρι είναι βρώμικο.	*to pot**ee**ree **ee**ne vromeek**o***

you may hear …

Ποιανού είναι το κοτόπουλο;	*peean**oo** **ee**ne to kot**o**poolo*	Who is the chicken for?
Όλα εντάξει;	***o**la end**a**ksee*	Everything all right?
Πώς είναι το ...;	*pos **ee**ne to*	How's the ...?
Σας αρέσει το φαγητό;	*sas ar**e**see to fayeet**o***	Are you enjoying your meal?

on your table

ashtray	το τασάκι	*to tasakee*
bowl	το μπολ	*to bol*
cup/glass	το φλυτζάνι/ποτήρι	*to fleedsanee/ poteeree*
fork	το πιρούνι	*to peeroonee*
knife	το μαχαίρι	*to maheree*
napkin	η πετσέτα	*ee petseta*
oil/vinegar	το λάδι/ξύδι	*to ladhee/kseedhee*
plate/dish	το πιάτο	*to peeato*
salt/pepper	το αλάτι/πιπέρι	*to alatee/peeperee*
spoon/teaspoon	το κουτάλι/κουταλάκι	*to kootalee/ kootalakee*
tablecloth	το τραπεζομάντηλο	*to trapezomandeelo*

paying the bill

you may say ...

The bill please.	Το λογαριασμό, παρακαλώ.	*to loghareeazmo parakalo*
Do you take credit cards?	Παίρνετε πιστωτικές κάρτες;	*pernete peestoteekes kartes*
Is service included?	Περιλαμβάνετε το φιλοδώρημα;	*pereelamvanete to feelodhoreema*
There's a mistake, I think.	Υπάρχει κάποιο λάθος νομίζω.	*eeparhee kapeeo lathos nomeezo*
We didn't have any beer/a dessert.	Δεν πήραμε μπύρα/ επιδόρπιο.	*dhen peerame beera/ epeedhorpeeo*
A receipt, please.	Μία απόδειξη, παρακαλώ.	*meea apodheeksee parakalo*
Keep the change.	Κρατήστε τα ρέστα.	*krateeste ta resta*

you may hear ...

Συγνώμη, δεχόμαστε μόνο μετρητά.	*seeghnomee dehomaste mono metreeta*	Sorry, we only accept cash.
Το φιλοδώρημα (δεν) περιλαμβάνεται.	*to feelodhoreema (dhen) pereelamvanete*	Service (isn't) included.

check out 3

Time to pay, but there's a problem with the bill.

- ❍ Όλα εντάξει;
  ola endaksee
- \- Υπάρχει κάποιο λάθος, νομίζω. Δεν πήραμε ρετσίνα.
  eeparhee kapeeo lathos nomeezo. dhen peerame retseena
- ❍ Συγνώμη. Ορίστε.
  seeghnomee. oreeste
- \- Ευχαριστώ. Θα ήθελα μία απόδειξη, παρακαλώ.
  efhareesto. tha eethela meea apodheeksee parakalo
- ❍ Μάλιστα.
  maleesta.

Q What were you charged for that you didn't have?

sound check

Notice the difference between these two similar sounds.

Δ, δ is pronounced like 'th' in 'that':
επιδόρπιο *epeedhorpeeo*

Θ, θ (th) is pronounced like 'th' in 'thin':
θέλω *thelo*

Practise on these words:

λάδι *ladhee*
λαδερά *ladhera*
θαλασσινά *thalaseena*
θα *tha*

try it out

mind the gap

Complete these sentences with the correct word from the list below. They're all things you might say in a restaurant.

1 Θέλω ένα ... για δύο
2 Έχει καμμιά καλή ... εδώ κοντά;
3 Ένα ... με ντομάτα και τζατζίκι.
4 Έχετε κόκκινο ... ;
5 Μία μπριζόλα και μία μερίδα ... παρακαλώ.
6 Ένα ποτήρι ... παρακαλώ.

a πατάτες
b νερό
c ταβέρνα
d τραπέζι
e σουβλάκι
f κρασί

as if you were there

You and your partner go into a fish restaurant in Kavala one evening. Follow the prompts to play your part.

Καλησπέρα σας.
*kaleesp**e**ra sas*
(Say good evening. Order some taramosalata and a portion of chips, then ask for feta cheese and a salad)
Μάλιστα. Τι θα πιείτε;
*m**a**leesta. tee tha pee**ee**te*
(Say, a bottle of red wine)
Δεν έχουμε κόκκινο κρασί.
*dhen **e**hoome k**o**keeno kras**ee***
(Now ask for a bottle of white wine)
Εντάξει.
*end**a**ksee*

linkup

Έχετε κατάλογο; ***e**hete kat**a**logho*	**Have you got** a menu?
Τι είναι παπουτσάκια; *tee **ee**ne papoots**a**keea*	**What is** 'παπουτσάκια'?
Μου φέρνετε μία ταραμοσαλάτα; *moo f**e**rnete m**ee**a taramosal**a**ta*	**(Will you) bring me** (a) taramosalata?
Θα πάρω ένα μουσακά. *tha p**a**ro **e**na moosak**a***	**I'll have** a moussaka.
Είμαι χορτοφάγος. ***ee**me hortof**a**ghos*	**I am** vegetarian.
Είναι κρύο. ***ee**ne kr**ee**o*	**It's** cold.

talking to 'you'

In Greek when talking to one person, there are two words for 'you':
Informally, for example when talking to one friend, a person you know fairly well, or a child, use εσύ *es**ee***.

When talking to a stranger, an elderly person or someone you want to be respectful towards, use the more formal εσείς *es**ee**s*.

This is also the plural form, used for addressing more than one person.

The word itself may often be missed out, but the one you choose determines the ending you put on the verb.

For example, a waiter would say to you:
Τι θα πάρετε; What will you have? (formal)
tee tha parete

But to a friend or someone you know fairly well you'd say:
Τι θα πάρεις; What will you have? (informal)
*tee tha p**a**rees*

When talking to a group of people the difference is not so obvious.
A waiter would ask a group of customers:
Τι θα πάρετε; What will you have? (plural)
*tee tha p**a**rete*
And you could ask your friends:
Τι θα πάρετε; What will you have? (plural)
*tee tha p**a**rete*

For notes on the 'formal' and 'informal' forms and using words like εσύ and εσείς, see Language Builder, p136.

Menu **Reader**

cooking styles

βραστός	*vrastos*	boiled
γεμιστός	*yemeestos*	stuffed
κοκκινιστός	*kokeeneestos*	in a tomato sauce
κρασάτος	*krasatos*	cooked in wine
λεμονάτος	*lemonatos*	in a lemon sauce
μαγειρευτός	*mayeerettos*	casseroled
μαρινάτος	*mareenatos*	marinated
στη σούβλα	*stee soovla*	spit roasted
στη σχάρα	*stee s-hara*	grilled
στο φούρνο	*sto foorno*	baked
τηγανητός	*teeghaneetos*	fried
ψητός	*pseetos*	roast
ωμός	*omos*	raw

the menu

αγγουροντομάτα	*angoorodomata*	cucumber and tomato salad
αθερίνα	*athereena*	whitebait
αστακός	*astakos*	lobster
αυγά	*avgha*	eggs
αχινός	*aheenos*	sea urchin
βλήτα	*vleeta*	dark green leaf vegetable
βύσσινο	*veeseeno*	sour cherry
γαρίδες	*ghareedhes*	shrimps
γεμιστά	*yemeesta*	stuffed peppers and tomatoes
γίγαντες	*yeeghandes*	giant broad beans in tomato sauce

γιουβαρλάκια	*yoovarl**a**keea*	meat and rice balls
γιουβέτσι	*yoov**e**tsee*	baked Greek pasta shapes
γκρέιπ φρουτ	*greee**p** froot*	grapefruit
γλυκά	*ghleek**a***	sweets
γλυκάδια	*ghleek**a**dhia*	sweetbread
γλώσσα	*ghl**o**sa*	sole
γόπες	*gh**o**pes*	large sardines
γουρουνόπουλο	*ghooroon**o**poolo*	suckling pig
γραβιέρα	*ghravee**e**ra*	Greek gruyere
γρανίτα	*ghran**ee**ta*	sherbet (crushed ice drink)
γύρος	*y**ee**ros*	doner kebab
δαμάσκηνο	*dham**a**skeeno*	plum
ελιές	*elee**e**s*	olives
επιδόρπιο	*epeedh**o**rpeeo*	dessert
ζυμαρικά	*zeemareek**a***	pasta
ιμάμ μπαϊλντί	*eem**a**m baeeld**ee***	stuffed aubergine
καβούρι	*kav**oo**ree*	crab
κακκαβιά	*kakavee**a***	spicy fish stew
καλαμαράκια	*kalamar**a**keea*	baby squid
καλαμάρι	*kalam**a**ree*	squid
καλαμπόκι	*kalamb**o**kee*	sweetcorn
καπνιστός	*kapneest**o**s*	smoked
καραβίδες	*karav**ee**dhes*	crawfish
καρύδι	*kar**ee**dhee*	walnut
κασέρι	*kas**e**ree*	hard yellow cheese
κατεψυγμένος	*katepseeghm**e**nos*	frozen

κατσίκι	*kats**ee**kee*	kid
κέφαλος	*k**e**falos*	mullet
κεφαλοτύρι	*kefalot**ee**ree*	salty yellow cheese
κεφτέδες	*keft**e**dhes*	meat balls
κιμάς	*keem**a**s*	mince
κοκοράκι	*kokor**a**kee*	capon
κοκορέτσι	*kokor**e**tsee*	grilled sheep's entrails
κομπόστα	*komb**o**sta*	stewed fruit
κοτόπιτα	*kot**o**peeta*	chicken pie
κουκιά	*kookee**a***	broad beans
κουνέλι	*koon**e**lee*	rabbit
κουνουπίδι	*koonoop**ee**dhee*	cauliflower
κουραμπιέδες	*koorabee**e**dhes*	almond cookies
κρεατόπιτα	*kreat**o**peeta*	meat pie
κρέμα καραμελέ	*kr**e**ma karamel**e***	crème caramel
κρεμμυδάκι	*kremeedh**a**kee*	spring onion
κυδώνι	*keedh**o**nee*	quince
κυνήγι	*keen**ee**yee*	game
λαγός	*lagh**o**s*	hare
λαδολέμονο	*ladhol**e**mono*	oil and lemon dressing
λαδόξιδο	*ladh**o**kseedho*	oil and vinegar dressing
λακέρδα	*lak**e**rdha*	salted tuna
λαχανικά	*lahaneek**a***	vegetables
λάχανο	*l**a**hano*	cabbage
λουκουμάδες	*lookoom**a**dhes*	honey fritters
λουκούμι	*look**oo**mee*	Turkish delight
λυθρίνι	*leethr**ee**nee*	gray mullet
μαγειρίτσα	*mayeer**ee**tsa*	Easter soup (of lamb's entrails)
μαγιονέζα	*mayon**e**za*	mayonnaise
μαϊντανός	*maeedan**o**s*	parsley
μακαρόνια	*makar**o**neea*	spaghetti
μανούρι	*man**oo**ree*	soft white cheese
μανταρίνι	*mandar**ee**nee*	mandarin
μαρίδες	*mar**ee**dhes*	(fried) smelt
μελομακάρονο	*melomak**a**rono*	small honey cakes
μερίδα	*mer**ee**dha*	portion

μήλο	meelo	apple
μηλόπιτα	meelopeeta	apple pie
μους	moos	mousse
μουσακάς	moosakas	moussaka
μουστάρδα	moostardha	mustard
μπάμια	bameea	okra
μπαρμπούνι	barboonee	red mullet
μπαχαρικά	bahareeka	spices
μπέικον	beeekon	bacon
μπιζέλια	beezeleea	petit pois
μπιφτέκι	beeftekee	grilled burger
μπουγάτσα	booghatsa	flaky pastry filled with custard
μπουρεκάκια	boorekakeea	small cheese pies (with meat)
μπούτι	bootee	leg
μπριάμ	breeam	ratatouille
μπριζόλες	breezoles	chops
μυαλά	meeala	brain
μύδια	meedheea	mussels
μυζήθρα	meezeethra	soft white cheese
νεφρά	nefra	kidneys
ντολμάδες	dolmadhes	stuffed vine/cabbage leaves
ξιφίας	kseefeeas	swordfish
ορεκτικά	orekteeka	starters
παγωμένος	paghomenos	chilled
παϊδάκια	paeedhakeea	lamb chops
παντζάρι	pandsaree	beetroot
παπάκι	papakee	duckling
πάπια	papia	duck
παπουτσάκια	papootsakeea	stuffed aubergines with béchamel
πάστα	pasta	cake
παστέλι	pastelee	sesame and honey bar
παστουρμάς	pastoormas	spiced cured meat
πατάτες τηγανητές	patates teeghaneetes	chips
πατάτες φούρνου	patates foornoo	oven-baked potatoes
πατέ	pate	pâté
πεπόνι	peponee	melon

πέρκα	*perka*	perch
πες μελμπά	*pes melba*	peach melba
πέστροφα	*pestrofa*	trout
πιλάφι	*peelafee*	pilau rice
πιπεριές (γεμιστές)	*peepereees (yemeestes)*	(stuffed) peppers
πλάτη	*platee*	shoulder
ποικιλία	*peekeeleea*	mixed hors d'oeuvres
πουρές	*poores*	mashed potato
πουτίγκα	*pooteega*	pudding
πράσα	*prasa*	leeks
πρασόρυζο	*prasoreezo*	leeks and rice
ραδίκια	*radheekeea*	dandelion
ραπανάκια	*rapanakeea*	radishes
ρεβίθια	*reveetheea*	chickpeas
ρόδι	*rodhee*	pomegranate
ρόκα	*roka*	rocket
ρυζόγαλο	*reezoghalo*	rice pudding
ρώσικη σαλάτα	*roseekee salata*	Russian salad
σαγανάκι	*saghanakee*	fried cheese
σαλάμι	*salamee*	salami
σαργός	*sarghos*	sea bream
σαρδέλα	*sardhela*	sardine
σέλινο	*seleeno*	celery
σκορδαλιά	*skordhaleea*	garlic and potato mash
σκουμπρί	*skoobree*	mackerel
σνίτσελ	*sneetsel*	schnitzel
σολομός	*solomos*	salmon
σουβλάκι	*soovlakee*	skewer
σούπα	*soopa*	soup
σουπιά	*soopeea*	cuttlefish
σουτζουκάκια	*soodsookakeea*	meatballs in sauce
σπανακόπιτα	*spanakopeeta*	spinach pie
σπανακόρυζο	*spanakoreezo*	spinach and rice
σπαράγγια	*sparangeea*	asparagus
σπετζοφάι	*spedsofaee*	spicy dish of sausage, peppers, etc.
σταφίδα	*stafeedha*	raisin
στιφάδο	*steefadho*	meat and onion stew

στρείδια	*str**ee**dheea*	oysters
σύκο	*s**ee**ko*	fig
συκώτι	*seek**o**tee*	liver
σφυρίδα	*sfeer**ee**dha*	grouper
ταραμοσαλάτα	*taramosal**a**ta*	fish-roe salad
τζατζίκι	*dsads**ee**kee*	yoghurt, cucumber and garlic dip
τόνος	*t**o**nos*	tuna
τοστ	*tost*	toasted sandwich
τουρσί	*toors**ee***	pickle
τούρτα σοκολάτα	*t**oo**rta sokol**a**ta*	chocolate cake
τριμμένος	*treem**e**nos*	grated
τσιπούρα	*tseep**oo**ra*	gilthead seabream
τσιπς	*tseeps*	crisps
τυρόπιτα	*teer**o**peeta*	cheese pie
φάβα	*f**a**va*	split peas (purée)
φαγκρί	*fagr**ee***	bream
φακές	*fak**e**s*	lentils
φασολάδα	*fasol**a**dha*	bean soup
φασολάκια	*fasol**a**keea*	green beans
φασόλια	*fas**o**leea*	haricot beans
φασόλια γιαχνί	*fas**o**leea yahn**ee***	beans in tomato sauce
φέτα	*f**e**ta*	ewe's milk cheese
φιλέτο	*feel**e**to*	fillet
φουντούκι	*foond**oo**kee*	hazelnut
φρικασέ	*freekas**e***	fricassée
φρούτα	*fr**oo**ta*	fruit
χαβιάρι	*havee**a**ree*	caviar
χαλβάς	*halv**a**s*	halva
χάμπουργκερ	*h**a**mboorger*	hamburger
χέλι	*h**e**lee*	eel
χόρτα	*h**o**rta*	wild greens
χουρμάς	*hoorm**a**s*	date
χταπόδι	*htap**o**dhee*	octopus
χυλοπίτες	*heelop**ee**tes*	noodles
χωριάτικη σαλάτα	*horee**a**teekee sal**a**ta*	Greek salad
ψαρόσουπα	*psar**o**soopa*	fish soup
ωμός	*om**o**s*	raw

(For drinks and more desserts, see Café Life, pp74-75.)

Entertainment

finding out what's on

Offices of EOT, the national tourist organisation, are found in all main towns and resorts, and can supply local maps, information and listings. English language newspapers, such as the weekly *Athens News*, are another good way to find out what's on; available at kiosks, or online at: **www.athensnews.gr**.

what to see

Football The Greeks never seem to get enough of this on television, and bars can be highly charged when a big match is on. For live football, the big teams are Panathinaikos and AEK in Athens, Olympiakos in Piraeus and PAOK of Thessaloniki, though most regional towns have their own teams. Basketball and volleyball are also hugely popular.

Music and dance Tourist resorts have made 'traditional Greek dancing' something of a cliché, but in fact Greek music remains extremely popular with the young and old alike. Try and visit a club specialising in **ρεμπέτικα** *rebeteeka*, one of the most evocative strands of Greek music.

Cinemas Most main towns have several cinemas showing films in their original version. In summer, open-air cinemas are an extremely atmospheric way of seeing a film.

Theatre Plays are often performed in Greece's classical theatres such as in Epidaurus and Athens. Though your Greek may not be up to understanding all performances, it is well worth a visit simply for the experience of being in the outdoor amphitheatre.

sports

Watersports You can windsurf at almost any resort or island around the country. Lessons for beginners make all the difference, and these are widely available and reasonably priced, as is board-hire. Waterskiing is almost as easy to find. Other common watersports are snorkelling and scuba diving, the latter prohibited in areas of underwater antiquities. Local diving schools and EOT offices can provide further details.

Golf courses exist in Corfu, Halkidiki, Rhodes, Crete and near Athens. You may need to show a Green Card or demonstrate a certain ability.

Yachting Captains and yachts can be hired at marinas around the country, such as at Glyfada, Varkiza and Vouliagmeni near Athens; Zea and Paleo Faliro in Piraeus; and those in Corfu, Halkidiki, Patra, Thessaloniki and Rhodes. Many coastal resorts also offer sailing instruction in daily or weekly courses, in group or private lessons. For more information see **www.sailing.gr**.

Skiing Though most visitors think of Greece as a summer destination, it is also possible to ski between December and April, although snow is not guaranteed at all times! The most popular destination is Mount Parnassos, near Delphi, others include: Helmos, Kalavrita in the Peloponnese; Velouhi in Karpenissi, Central Greece; Hania in the Pelion; Mount Falakron near Drama and Pisodheri near Florina, Macedonia.

Trekking A highly recommended way to see parts of the country not covered by package deal operators. Specialist travel agents organise treks of varying length and ease over hill and mountain country on the mainland and some islands. However, most of inland Greece and the Greek islands themselves offer plenty to walkers of any ability. Try and stick to established footpaths and get a good map, as some of Greece is extremely mountainous and remote and subject to sudden weather changes; take care in gorges, which are prone to flash floods outside summer.

Adventure sports Sports such as mountain biking, hang-gliding, caving, canyoning, para-gliding, kayaking and rafting are increasingly popular. Most of mainland Greece forms a natural playground of mountains and shallow rivers descending in rapids, and adventure packages are run by private tour operators and local authorities. Some sports are only offered in winter months.

Mountaineering can be dangerous, especially in winter, and should be carefully planned. Information on routes and trails, alpine refuges and local climbing conditions can be found at **www.oreivatein.com**, the website of the Greek Mountaineering and Rock-Climbing Association, who also organise climbing expeditions.

children

Children are held in high esteem in Greece and are welcome everywhere. The Children's Museum in Plaka, Athens, has special activities designed to amuse and inform, and playgrounds are found in almost every neighbourhood around the country. However, changing facilities within shopping areas and restaurants can be scarce.

phrasemaker

finding out what's on

you may say ...

Do you have ...	Έχετε ...	*ehete*
a map of the town?	χάρτη της πόλης;	*hartee tees polees*
an entertainment guide?	έναν οδηγό διασκέδασης;	*enan odheegho dheeaskedhasees*
Do you have any information in English?	Έχετε πληροφορίες στα Αγγλικά;	*ehete pleeroforeees sta angleeka*
What is there to see/do here?	Τι έχει να δούμε/ κάνουμε εδώ;	*tee ehee na dhoome/ kanoome edho*
Is there ...	Υπάρχει ...	*eeparhee*
a guided tour?	ξενάγηση με ξεναγό;	*ksenayeesee me ksenagho*
a bus tour?	ξενάγηση με λεωφορείο;	*ksenayeesee me leoforeeo*
Is there ... here?	Υπάρχει (έχει) ... εδώ;	*eeparhee (ehee) edho*
a cinema	σινεμά	*seenema*
a nightclub	κλαμπ	*klab*
a tourist information office	γραφείο τουρισμού του ΕΟΤ	*ghrafeeo tooreesmoo too e o t*
a swimming pool	πισίνα	*peeseena*
Can you recommend ...	Μπορείτε να μας συστήσετε ...	*boreete na mas seesteesete*
a restaurant?	ένα εστιατόριο;	*ena esteeatoreeo*
an exhibition?	κάποια έκθεση;	*kapeea ekthesee*
I like ...	Μ' αρέσει ...	*maresee*
modern art.	η μοντέρνα τέχνη.	*ee moderna tehnee*
football.	το ποδόσφαιρο.	*to podhosfero*

you may hear ...

Τι σας ενδιαφέρει;	*tee sas endheeaferee*	What are you interested in?
Υπάρχει ξενάγηση με ξεναγό.	*eeparhee ksenayeesee me ksenagho*	There is a guided tour.

getting more information

you may say ...

Where is ...	Πού είναι ...	*poo **ee**ne*
the (art) gallery?	η γκαλερί;	*ee galer**ee***
the public gallery?	η πινακοθήκη;	*ee peenakoth**ee**kee*
the castle?	το κάστρο;	*to k**a**stro*
the theatre?	το θέατρο;	*to th**e**atro*
the concert hall?	η αίθουσα συναυλιών;	*ee **e**thoosa seenavlee**o**n*
Where does the tour start?	Πού αρχίζει η ξενάγηση;	*poo arh**ee**zee ee ksen**a**yeesee*
What time does it start/finish?	Τι ώρα αρχίζει/ τελειώνει;	*tee **o**ra arh**ee**zee/ teleе**o**nee*
What time does it open/close?	Τι ώρα ανοίγει/ κλείνει;	*tee **o**ra an**ee**yee/ kl**ee**nee*
What time does it leave/get back?	Τι ώρα φεύγει/ επιστρέφει;	*tee **o**ra f**e**vyee/ epeestr**e**fee*
How long does it last?	Πόση ώρα κρατάει;	*p**o**see **o**ra krata**ee***
Where does the bus leave from?	Από πού φεύγει το λεωφορείο;	*ap**o** poo f**e**vyee to leofor**ee**o*

Is there wheelchair access?	Υπάρχει πρόσβαση για άτομα με αναπηρίες;	*eeparhee prozvasee ya atoma me anapeereees*
Is there anything for the children to do?	Υπάρχει κάτι να κάνουν τα παιδιά;	*eeparhee katee na kanoon ta pedheea*
Do you need tickets?	Χρειάζονται εισιτήρια;	*hreeazonde eeseeteereea*
Where can I buy tickets?	Πού μπορώ να αγοράσω εισιτήρια;	*poo boro na aghoraso eeseeteereea*
Is it open ... on Mondays? at the weekend?	Είναι ανοιχτά ... τις Δευτέρες; το Σαββατοκύριακο;	*eene aneehta* *tees defteres* *to savatokeereeako*

you may hear ...

Το λεωφορείο φεύγει στις/από ...	*to leoforeeo fevyee stees/apo*	The bus leaves at/ from ...
Το μουσείο είναι ... ανοιχτό κάθε μέρα. κλειστό τις Κυριακές. ανοιχτό από τις δέκα μέχρι τις έξι.	*to mooseeo eene* *aneehto kathe mera* *kleesto tees keereeakes* *aneehto apo tees dheka mehree tees eksee*	The museum is ... open every day. closed on Sundays. open from 10am to 6pm.
Μπορείτε να αγοράσετε εισιτήρια ... εδώ. στο εκδοτήριο.	*boreete na aghorasete eseeteereea* *edho* *sto ekdhoteereeo*	You can buy the tickets ... here. at the ticket office.
Δεν χρειάζεστε εισιτήρια.	*dhen hreeazeste eeseeteereea*	You don't need tickets.
Στην κεντρική πλατεία στις δέκα.	*steen kendreekee plateea stees dheka*	In the main square, at 10 o'clock.
Ορίστε ... στο χάρτη στο σχέδιο	*oreeste* *ston hartee* *sto s-hedheeo*	Here ... on the map. on the plan.
Υπάρχει παιδική χαρά.	*eeparhee pedheekee hara*	There is a playground.

Entertainment

check out 1

You are in the tourist office, asking about a guided tour of the town.

- ❍ Υπάρχει ξενάγηση με ξεναγό;
  *eep**a**rhee ksen**a**yeesee me ksenagh**o***
- \- Μάλιστα.
  *m**a**leesta*
- ❍ Τι ώρα αρχίζει;
  *tee **o**ra arh**ee**zee*
- \- Στις δώδεκα.
  *stees dh**o**dheka*

Q What time does the tour start?

things to do or see

antiquities	οι αρχαιότητες/τα αρχαία	*ee arhe**o**teetes/ta arh**e**a*
beach	η πλαζ/η παραλία	*ee plaz/ee paral**ee**a*
castle	το κάστρο	*to k**a**stro*
cathedral	η μητρόπολη	*ee meetr**o**polee*
church	η εκκλησία	*ee eklees**ee**a*
cinema	ο κινηματογράφος /το σινεμά	*o keeneematoghr**a**fos /to seenem**a***
concert	η συναυλία	*ee seenavl**ee**a*
festival	η γιορτή/το φεστιβάλ	*ee yort**ee**/to festeev**a**l*
film	η ταινία	*ee ten**ee**a*
fireworks	τα πυροτεχνήματα	*ta peerotehn**ee**mata*
football/basketball match	αγώνας ποδοσφαίρου/ μπάσκετ	*agh**o**nas podhosf**e**roo/b**a**sket*
monastery	το μοναστήρι	*to monast**ee**ree*
museum	το μουσείο	*to moos**ee**o*
play	το θεατρικό έργο	*to theatreek**o** **e**rgho*
show	το πρόγραμμα	*to pr**o**ghrama*
stadium	το στάδιο/το γήπεδο	*to st**a**dheeo/ to y**ee**pedo*

buying a ticket

you may say ...

Do you have any tickets?	Έχετε εισιτήρια;	ehete eeseeteereea
How much is it?	Πόσο κάνει;	poso kanee
Two tickets, please.	Δύο εισιτήρια, παρακαλώ.	dheeo eeseeteereea parakalo
for ... Saturday tomorrow	για ... το Σάββατο αύριο	ya to savato avreeo
Are there any concessions?	Υπάρχει κάποια έκπτωση;	eeparhee kapeea ekptosee
How long does it last?	Πόση ώρα κρατάει;	posee ora krataee
Does the film have subtitles in English?	Έχει η ταινία υπότιτλους στα Αγγλικά;	ehee ee teneea eepoteetloos sta angleeka
Is there ... a programme? a cloakroom?	Υπάρχει ... πρόγραμμα; βεστιάριο;	eeparhee proghrama vesteeareeo
Is there an interval?	Κάνει διάλειμμα;	kanee dheealeema
Are the seats numbered?	Είναι αριθμημένες οι θέσεις;	eene areethmeemenes ee thesees
Is this place taken?	Είναι πιασμένη η θέση;	eene peeazmenee ee thesee

you may hear ...

Ναι, για ... φοιτητές. παιδιά. συνταξιούχους.	*ne ya* *feeteet**e**s* *pedhee**a*** *seendakseeo**o**hoos*	Yes, for ... students. children. pensioners.
Συγνώμη, τελείωσαν.	*seeghn**o**mee tel**ee**osan*	Sorry, it's sold out.
ένα διάλειμμα είκοσι λεπτών	***e**na dhee**a**leema **ee**kosee lept**o**n*	one interval of 20 minutes
Είναι ελεύθερη/ πιασμένη.	*eene el**e**ftheree/ peeazm**e**nee*	It's free/taken.
Μπορείτε να καθίσετε όπου θέλετε.	*bor**ee**te na kath**ee**sete **o**poo th**e**lete*	You can sit where you like.
εδώ/εκεί	*edh**o**/ek**ee***	here/over there
πλατεία/εξώστης/ δεύτερος εξώστης	*plat**ee**a/eks**o**stees/ dh**e**fteros eks**o**stees*	stall/circle/balcony

check out 2

You are finding out about concert tickets.

○ Πότε είναι η συναυλία παρακαλώ;
*p**o**te **ee**ne ee seenavl**ee**a parakal**o***

- Την Τετάρτη.
*teen tet**a**rtee*

○ Έχει εισιτήρια;
***e**hee eeseet**ee**reea*

- Μάλιστα.
*m**a**leesta*

○ Πόσο κάνουν;
*p**o**so k**a**noon*

- Σαράντα ευρώ.
*sar**a**nda evr**o***

Q Which day does the concert take place?
It's sold out: true or false?

swimming & sunbathing

you may say ...

Can I use the hotel pool?	Μπορώ να χρησιμοποιήσω την πισίνα το ξενοδοχείου;	*bor**o** na hreeseemopee**ee**so teen pees**ee**na too ksenodhoh**ee**oo*
Where are ...	Πού είναι ...	*poo **ee**ne*
the changing rooms?	τα αποδυτήρια;	*ta apodheet**ee**reea*
the showers?	τα ντους;	*ta doos*
Where can I go swimming?	Πού μπορώ να πάω για μπάνιο;	*poo bor**o** na p**a**o ya b**a**neeo*
I'd like to hire ...	Θα ήθελα να νοικιάσω ...	*tha **ee**thela na neekee**a**so*
a beach umbrella.	μία ομπρέλα.	*m**ee**a ombr**e**la*
a sunlounger.	μία ξαπλώστρα.	*m**ee**a ksapl**o**stra*
a towel.	μία πετσέτα.	*m**ee**a pets**e**ta*

signs

you may see ...

απαγορεύεται το κολύμπι	no swimming
ναυαγοσώστης	lifeguard
ιδιωτική πλαζ	private beach
κίνδυνος	danger
πρώτες βοήθειες	first aid

sports

you may say ...

Where can I ...	Πού μπορώ να ...	*poo boro na*
play tennis/golf/ volleyball?	παίξω τένις/γκολφ/ μπιτς βόλεϊ;	*pekso tenees/golf/ beets volee*
go fishing?	πάω για ψάρεμα;	*pao ya psarema*
go riding?	κάνω ιππασία;	*kano eepaseea*
go climbing?	κάνω ορειβασία;	*kano oreevaseea*
go walking?	πάω για πεζοπορία;	*pao ya pezoporeea*
watch basketball/ football?	δω μπάσκετ/ ποδόσφαιρο;	*dho basket/ podhosfero*
I'd like to hire ...	Θα ήθελα να νοικιάσω ...	*tha eethela na neekeeaso*
a racket.	μία ρακέτα.	*meea raketa*
(water)skis.	σκι.	*skee*
a bike.	ένα ποδήλατο.	*ena podheelato*
I'd like to take ... lessons.	Θα ήθελα να κάνω μαθήματα ...	*tha eethela na kano matheemata*
windsurfing	γουίντ σέρφινγκ/ ιστιοσανίδας.	*ghooeend serfeeng/ eesteeosaneedhas*
surfing	σέρφινγκ.	*serfeeng*
sailing	ιστιοπλοΐας.	*eesteeoploeeas*
scuba diving	καταδύσεων.	*katadheeseon*
skiing	σκι.	*skee*
Can children do it too?	Μπορούν να το κάνουν και τα παιδιά;	*boroon na to kanoon ke ta pedheea*
How much is it per ...	Πόσο κάνει/ στοιχίζει ...	*poso kanee/ steeheezee*
hour?	την ώρα;	*teen ora*
day?	την ημέρα;	*teen eemera*

you may hear ...

Είστε αρχάριος (m)/ αρχάρια (f);	*eeste arhareeos/ arhareea*	Are you a beginner?
Κάνει/κοστίζει ... την ώρα/ημέρα.	*kanee/kosteezee teen ora/eemera*	It's ... per hour/day.

sports equipment

boat	το σκάφος	*to sk**a**fos*
boots	οι μπότες	*ee b**o**tes*
dinghy/sailing boat	το καΐκι	*to ka**ee**kee*
golf clubs	τα μπαστούνια του γκολφ	*ta bast**oo**neea too golf*
life belt	η ζώνη ασφαλείας	*ee z**o**nee asfal**ee**as*
rubber dinghy	η λαστιχένια βάρκα	*ee lasteeh**e**neea v**a**rka*
skates	τα πατίνια	*ta pat**ee**neea*
skis	τα σκι	*ta skee*
snowboard	το σνόουμπορντ	*to sn**o**ooboard*
tennis racket/balls	οι ρακέτες/μπάλες του τένις	*ee rak**e**tes/b**a**les too t**e**nees*
(wind)surf board	το σερφ/η ιστιοσανίδα	*to serf/ee eesteeosan**ee**dha*

check out 3

You ask about playing tennis.

○ Γεια σας. Τι ώρα μπορώ να παίξω τένις;
*ya sas. tee **o**ra bor**o** na p**e**kso t**e**nees*

\- Στις τέσσερεις ή στις έξι.
*stees t**e**serees ee stees **e**ksee*

○ Στις έξι. Θα ήθελα να νοικιάσω δύο ρακέτες.
*stees **e**ksee. tha **ee**thela na neekee**a**so dh**ee**o rak**e**tes*

\- Μάλιστα. Δεκαπέντε ευρώ.
*m**a**leesta. dhekap**e**nde evr**o***

Q What times are available?

sound check

η, ι, υ, οι, ει and **υι** – these six vowels, or combinations of vowels, are all pronounced similarly to the 'ee' in 'meet', but clipped short.

πόλη *p**o**lee*
υπάρχει *eep**a**rhee*
έχει ***e**hee*
τι *tee*
νοικιάσω *neekee**a**so*

Practise on these words:

αρχίζει *arh**ee**zee*
δύο *dh**ee**o*
συστήσετε *seest**ee**sete*
ξενάγηση *ksen**a**yeesee*
εισιτήρια *eeseet**ee**reea*

try it out

in the mix

Rearrange the letters in the following words to form places you might want to visit, e.g. οεμίσυο = μουσείο.

1 θινήκκπηαο **2** ορτθέα **3** αρπαλία
4 σίιπνα **5** λακπμ

as if you were there

On holiday on Crete, you go into the Tourist Office to get some information about dance performance at a local club. Follow the prompts to play your part.

(Ask what time the nightclub opens)
Στις εννιά.
(Ask what time the show starts)
Στις δώδεκα.
(Ask if you need tickets)
Δεν χρειάζεστε.
(Say thank you)

linkup

key phrases

Έχετε φυλλάδια στ' Αγγλικά; *eehete feeladheea stangleeka*	**Do you have** any leaflets in English?
Υπάρχει ξενάγηση; *eeparhee ksenayeesee*	**Is there** a guided tour?
Πού μπορώ να αγοράσω εισιτήρια; *poo boro na agoraso eeseeteereeo*	**Where can I** buy tickets?
Θα ήθελα να νοικιάσω μία ρακέτα. *tha eethela na neekeeaso meea raketa*	**I'd like to** hire a racket.

more than one

To talk about more than one of something, there are various patterns you can follow for changing the word ending.

For example, masculine words ending in **-ος** change to **-οι**:
δρόμος *dhromos* road > δρόμοι *dhromee* roads
Feminine words ending in **-α** change to **-ες**:
πισίνα *peeseena* pool > πισίνες *peeseenes* pools
Neuter words ending in **-ο** change to **-α**:
μουσείο *mooseeo* museum > μουσεία *mooseea* museums

Words 'borrowed' from English, which are always neuter, have no change in the plural, e.g. μπαρ *bar* bar; μπαρ *bar* bars.

If you're asking for more than one of something in Greek, you don't need a word for 'some' or 'any'.
Έχετε εισιτήρια για φοιτητές; Do you have (any) tickets for students? *ehete eeseeteereea ya feeteetes*
Πού έχει μπάλες για τένις; Where are there (some) tennis balls? *poo ehee bales ya tenees*

For more on plurals, see the Language Builder, p133.

Emergencies

reporting crime

Crime rates in Greece are comfortingly low. Greeks are particularly honest when it comes to personal belongings, usually leaving things unattended on beaches etc., although it is better not to tempt fate in tourist areas.

If you do have anything stolen or need the police, go to the **αστυνομικό τμήμα** *asteenomeek**o** tm**ee**ma* (local police station) or contact the tourist police, who speak various languages.

The commonest source of complaints stems from taxi drivers over-charging, particularly from airports. Look out for a list of approximate rates before leaving the terminal. If you feel there is a serious problem, tell the driver to drive to the nearest police station. This will usually settle the issue.

health

Most regions have local state hospitals and health centres, although the latter are basic. For out-of-hours emergency treatment in places with more than one state hospital, go to the **εφημερεύον** *efeemer**e**von* (duty hospital). In larger cities on the mainland, there are private hospitals that offer a faster treatment for non-emergencies; ask the tourist police.

EU nationals must have a valid European Health Insurance Card (EHIC) entitling them to free or free emergency treatment in Greek state hospitals, available from UK post offices, or online: **www.dh.gov.uk/travellers**.

Φαρμακείο *farmak**ee**o* (chemist's) can help you with everyday medical problems and most medicines can be issued without a prescription. In every town there is a duty chemist open at all times; check other chemists' windows for details.

The single biggest enemy to your health in Greece is its number one attraction, the sun. Tap water is generally fine to drink, though on some islands (such as Santorini) it is saline.

Bottled water is cheaply available everywhere. There are venomous adders in Greece but they are not found in abundance. Scorpions are even rarer but are poisonous. In the unlikely event of being bitten or stung, medical help should be sought without delay. Jellyfish and sea urchins are a minor hazard when swimming. Toilets are labelled **Ανδρών** *andhr**o**n* for men and **Γυναικών** *yeenek**o**n* for women.

travellers with disabilities

Wheelchair access is improving all over Greece, particularly in Athens since the 2004 Olympics. The new airport and the metro system are wheelchair accessible, and a lift can take wheelchair users to the top of the Acropolis. Modern and private facilities are gradually beginning to provide ramps and disabled bathrooms, but checking ahead with your accommodation about any specific requirements is always recommended.

post offices

Most **ταχυδρομεία** *taheedhrom**ee**a* (post offices) open Monday to Friday from 8am to 2pm, and some city branches remain open until 8pm and at weekends. **Γραμματόσημα** *ghramat**o**seema* (stamps) can also be bought from **περίπτερο** *per**ee**ptero* (kiosks) though you'll pay slightly more than you would at a post office. Post letters in the yellow post boxes; some have a separate slot marked **εξωτερικό** *eksotereek**o*** for overseas mail.

breakdowns

Most car hire companies have arrangements with road assistance organisations such as Express Service (telephone 1154). Check with your hire company. If you take your own car, check before travelling to see if your breakdown service has a reciprocal agreement with ELPA (telephone 104 00).

making phone calls

Public phones are plentiful; all require **τηλεκάρτα** *teelek**a**rta* (phonecards), which are available from kiosks, mini-markets and Hellenic Telecommunications Organization (OTE) offices. Simply insert your card and dial. OTE offices are useful for long distance calls, and can be found in most towns and villages. Hotels charge rates well above the norm, so use outside phones to keep your bills down.

You'll find an **ίντερνετ καφέ** *eenternet kafe* (internet café) in most areas, while Wi-Fi hotspots are becoming more common, especially in cafés, hotels and stations. Look for relevant signs.

useful phone numbers

Phone numbers in Greece are ten digits, with no local dialling code. The country code is +30.

Directory enquiries 118 88

International directory enquiries 139

Emergency services 112. (An operator will then connect you to ambulance, fire service, police etc.)

Tourist Police 171 (for minor tourist-related problems or advice in English)

Coast guard/Port police 108

Poisoning Treatment Centre 210 7793777

SOS Iatroi 1016 (24-hour Private Medical Service in Athens)

Holiday and Night Duty Hospitals, Doctors and Chemists 1434

phrasemaker

emergency phrases

you may say ...

Help!	Βοήθεια!	*voeetheea*
Excuse me!/ Hello there! (to attract attention)	Συγνώμη!	*seeghnomee*
Thank you!	Ευχαριστώ!	*efhareesto*
Can you help me?	Μπορείτε να με βοηθήσετε;	*boreete na me voeetheesete*
I've had an accident.	Έπαθα ένα ατύχημα.	*epatha ena ateeheema*
Where is the nearest ...	Πού είναι το πιο κοντινό ...	*poo eene to peeo kondeeno*
petrol station?	βενζινάδικο;	*venzeenadheeko*
garage?	συνεργείο;	*seeneryeeo*
hospital?	νοσοκομείο;	*nosokomeeo*
chemist's?	φαρμακείο;	*farmakeeo*
police station?	αστυνομικό τμήμα;	*asteenomeeko tmeema*
casualty department?	τμήμα επειγόντων περιστατικών;	*tmeema epeeghondon pereestateekon*
I need ...	Χρειάζομαι ...	*hreeazome*
a doctor.	γιατρό.	*yatro*
an ambulance.	ασθενοφόρο.	*asthenoforo*
a telephone.	τηλέφωνο.	*teelefono*
Is there someone here who speaks English?	Μιλάει κανένας εδώ Αγγλικά;	*meelaee kanenas edho angleeka*
It's urgent.	Είναι επείγον.	*eene epeeghon*
Leave me alone!	Αφήστε με ήσυχο (m)/ήσυχη (f)!	*afeeste me eeseeho/ eeseehee*
I'll call the police.	Θα φωνάξω την αστυνομία.	*tha fonakso teen asteenomeea*

saying what's wrong

you may say ...

I'd like an appointment with ...	Θέλω να κλείσω ραντεβού με ...	*th**e**lo na kl**ee**so randev**oo** me*
a doctor.	το γιατρό.	*to yatr**o***
a dentist.	τον οδοντογιατρό.	*ton odhondoyatr**o***
My ... hurts.	Πονάει ...	*pon**a**ee*
stomach	το στομάχι μου.	*to stom**a**hee moo*
head	το κεφάλι μου.	*to kef**a**lee moo*
tooth	το δόντι μου.	*to dh**o**ndee moo*
My eyes hurt.	Πονάνε τα μάτια μου.	*pon**a**ne ta m**a**teea moo*
It hurts here.	Πονάει εδώ.	*pon**a**ee edh**o***
I'm in a lot of pain.	Πονάω πολύ.	*pon**a**o pol**ee***
I can't move ...	Δεν μπορώ να κουνήσω ...	*dhen bor**o** na koon**ee**so*
my neck.	το λαιμό μου.	*to lem**o** moo*
my lower back.	τη μέση μου.	*tee m**e**see moo*
I can't feel ...	Δεν αισθάνομαι ...	*dhen esth**a**nome*
my leg.	το πόδι μου.	*to p**o**dhee moo*
my arm.	το χέρι μου.	*to h**e**ree moo*
I can't breathe.	Δεν μπορώ να αναπνεύσω.	*den bor**o** na anapn**e**fso*
My son/My daughter has a temperature.	Ο γιος μου/Η κόρη μου έχει πυρετό.	*o yos moo/ee k**o**ree moo **e**hee peeret**o***
He/She feels ill.	Δεν αισθάνεται καλά.	*dhen esth**a**nete kal**a***
I've got ...	Έχω ...	***e**ho*
constipation.	δυσκοιλιότητα.	*dheeskeelee**o**teeta*
diarrhoea.	διάρροια.	*dee**a**reea*
a cough.	βήχα.	*v**ee**ha*
a headache.	πονοκέφαλο.	*ponok**e**falo*
hayfever.	αλλεργία στη γύρη.	*alery**ee**a stee y**ee**ree*
a sore throat.	το λαιμό μου.	*to lem**o** moo*
I have a cold.	Είμαι κρυωμένος/ κρυωμένη.	*eeme kreeom**e**nos/ kreeom**e**nee*
I feel sick.	Έχω τάση για εμετό.	***e**ho t**a**see ya emet**o***
I've been sick.	Έκανα εμετό.	***e**kana emet**o***

I've cut/burnt myself.	Κόπηκα/Κάηκα.	*k**o**peeka/k**a**eeka*
I've been bitten by a dog.	Με δάγκωσε σκύλος.	*me dh**a**ngose sk**ee**los*
I've been stung by an insect.	Με τσίμπησε έντομο.	*me ts**ee**beese **e**ndomo*
I'm allergic to ...	Είμαι αλλεργικός ...	***ee**me aleryeek**o**s*
cats.	στις γάτες.	*stees gh**a**tes*
antibiotics.	στα αντιβιοτικά.	*sta andeeveeoteek**a***
nuts.	στους ξηρούς καρπούς.	*stoos kseer**oo**s karp**oo**s*
dairy.	στα γαλακτοκομικά.	*sta galaktokomeek**a***
wheat.	στα προϊόντα σίτου.	*sta proee**o**nda s**ee**too*
seafood.	στα θαλασσινά.	*sta thalaseen**a***
penicillin.	στην πενικιλίνη.	*steen peneekeel**ee**nee*
cortisone.	στην κορτιζόνη.	*steen korteez**o**nee*
I'm ...	Είμαι ...	***ee**me*
diabetic.	διαβητικός (m)/ διαβητική (f).	*dheeaveeteek**o**s/ dheeaveeteek**ee***
pregnant.	έγκυος.	***e**ngeeos*
epileptic.	επιληπτικός.	*epeeleepteek**o**s*
HIV positive.	φορέας του HIV.	*for**e**as too HIV*
I have ...	Έχω ...	***e**ho*
asthma.	άσθμα.	***a**s-thma*
high/low blood pressure.	υψηλή/χαμηλή πίεση.	*eepseel**ee**/hameel**ee** p**ee**esee*
I have a heart condition.	Έχω καρδιακή πάθηση.	***e**ho kardheeak**ee** p**a**theesee*
I have toothache.	Έχω πονόδοντο.	***e**ho pon**o**dhondo*
I've broken a tooth.	Έσπασα ένα δόντι.	***e**spasa **e**na dh**o**ndee*
I've lost ...	Μου έπεσε ...	*moo **e**pese*
a filling.	ένα σφράγισμα.	***e**na sfr**a**yeezma*
a crown.	μία κορώνα.	*m**ee**a kor**o**na*
I have a European Health Insurance Card.	Έχω Ευρωπαϊκή Κάρτα Ασφάλισης Υγείας.	***e**ho evropaeek**ee** k**a**rta asf**a**leesees eey**ee**as*

you may hear …

Πώς αισθάνεστε;	*pos esthaneste*	How are you feeling?
Πού πονάει;	*poo ponaee*	Where does it hurt?
Παίρνετε κάποιο φάρμακο;	*pernete kapeeo farmako*	Are you on medication?
Είστε αλλεργικός σε κάτι;	*eeste aleryeekos se katee*	Are you allergic to anything?
Τι φάγατε/ήπιατε;	*tee faghate/eepeeate*	What have you eaten/drunk?
Έχετε πάθει τροφική δηλητηρίαση.	*ehete pathee trofeekee deeleeteereeasee*	It's food poisoning.
Δεν είναι σοβαρό.	*dhen eene sovaro*	It's not serious.
Το κόκαλο είναι σπασμένο.	*to kokalo eene spazmeno*	The bone is broken.
Είναι διάστρεμμα.	*eene dheeastrema*	It's a sprain.
Έχει μολυνθεί.	*ehee moleenthee*	It's infected.
Θα χρειαστεί εγχείριση.	*tha hreeastee enheereesee*	You will need an operation.
Χρειάζεται να κάνετε ακτινογραφία.	*hreeazete na kanete akteenoghrafeea*	You need an X-ray.
Πρέπει να …	*prepee na*	You must …
πατε στο νοσοκομείο.	*pate sto nosokomeeo*	go to hospital.
μείνετε στο κρεβάτι.	*meenete sto krevatee*	stay in bed.
αναπαυθείτε.	*anapaftheete*	rest.
πίνετε πολλά υγρά.	*peenete pola eeghra*	drink lots of water.
Ορίστε η συνταγή.	*oreeste ee seentayee*	This is a prescription.
Θα σας βάλω ένα (προσωρινό) σφράγισμα.	*tha sas valo ena (prosoreeno) sfrayeezma*	I'll put in a (temporary) filling.
Πρέπει να βγάλω αυτό το δόντι.	*prepee na vghalo afto to dhondee*	I'll have to take this tooth out.

at the chemist's

you may say ...

Do you have something for ...	Έχετε κάτι για ...	*ehete katee ya*
a cold?	το κρυολόγημα;	*to kreeoloyeema*
a cough?	το βήχα;	*to veeha*
diarrhoea?	τη διάρροια;	*tee dheeareea*
sunburn?	το έγκαυμα από τον ήλιο;	*to engavma apo ton eeleeo*
constipation?	τη δυσκοιλιότητα;	*tee dheeskeeleeoteeta*
burns?	τα εγκαύματα;	*ta engavmata*
insect stings?	τα τσιμπήματα;	*ta tseebeemata*
Do you have any ...	Έχετε ...	*ehete*
antihistamine?	αντιισταμινικό;	*andee-eestameeneeko*
aspirin?	ασπιρίνες;	*aspeereenes*
baby food?	βρεφική τροφή;	*vrefeekee trofee*
condoms?	προφυλακτικά;	*profeelakteeka*
cough mixture?	σιρόπι για το βήχα;	*seeropee ya to veeha*
insect repellent?	εντομοαπωθητικό;	*endomoapotheeteeko*

you may hear ...

Πάρτε/Βάλτε ...	*parte/valte*	Take/Apply ...
αυτό το φάρμακο.	*afto to farmako*	this medicine.
αυτή την αλοιφή/ κρέμα.	*aftee teen aleefee/ krema*	this ointment/ cream.
αυτά τα χάπια/ αντιβιοτικά.	*afta ta hapeea/ andeeveeoteeka*	these pills/ antibiotics.
... την ημέρα	*... teen eemera*	... a day
μία φορά	*meea fora*	once
δύο φορές	*dheeo fores*	twice
τρεις φορές	*trees fores*	three times
πριν/μετά το φαγητό	*preen/meta to fayeeto*	before/after meals
με νερό	*me nero*	with water
Μασήστε, μην καταπίνετε.	*maseeste, meen katapeenete*	Chew, don't swallow whole.

check out 1

You are suffering from diarrhoea, and go to the chemist's for help.

- Έχετε κάτι για τη διάρροια;
  ehete katee ya tee dheeareea
- Πάρτε αυτά τα χάπια. Τρεις φορές την ημέρα.
  parte afta ta hapeea. trees fores teen eemera
- Πότε;
  pote
- Πριν το φαγητό.
  preen to fayeeto

Q How often do you have to take the tablets?
You have to take them after meals: true or false?

toiletries

after-sun lotion	γαλάκτωμα για μετά τον ήλιο	*ghalaktoma ya meta ton eeleeo*
hair conditioner	κρέμα μαλλιών	*krema maleeon*
contact lens solution	υγρό φακών επαφής	*eeghro fakon epafees*
deodorant	αποσμητικό	*apozmeeteeko*
moisturiser	ενυδατική κρέμα	*eneedhateekee krema*
nappies	πάνες	*panes*
plasters	χανζαπλάστ	*hanzaplast*
sanitary towels	σερβιέτες	*serveeetes*
shampoo	σαμπουάν	*sampooan*
shaving cream	αφρός ξυρίσματος	*afros kseereezmatos*
soap	σαπούνι	*sapoonee*
sun lotion	αντιηλιακό	*andeeleeako*
tampons	ταμπόν	*tabon*
toothbrush	οδοντόβουρτσα	*odhondovoortsa*
toothpaste	οδοντόκρεμα	*odhondokrema*

parts of the body

ankle	ο αστράγαλος	*o astr**a**ghalos*
arm	το χέρι	*to h**e**ree*
back	η πλάτη	*ee pl**a**tee*
chest	το στήθος	*to st**ee**thos*
inner/outer ear	το εσωτερικό/ εξωτερικό αυτί	*to esotereek**o**/ eksotereek**o** aft**ee***
eye/eyes	το μάτι/τα μάτια	*to m**a**tee/ta m**a**teea*
finger	το δάχτυλο	*to dh**a**hteelo*
foot	το πόδι	*to p**o**dhee*
hand/hands	το χέρι/τα χέρια	*to h**e**ree/ta h**e**reea*
head	το κεφάλι	*to kef**a**lee*
heart	η καρδιά	*ee kardhee**a***
hip	ο γοφός	*o ghof**o**s*
kidneys	τα νεφρά	*ta nefr**a***
knee	το γόνατο	*to gh**o**nato*
leg/legs	το πόδι/τα πόδια	*to p**o**dhee/ta p**o**dia*
liver	το συκώτι	*to seek**o**tee*
neck	ο λαιμός	*o lem**o**s*
nose	η μύτη	*ee m**ee**tee*
toe/toes	το δάχτυλο/τα δάχτυλα	*to dh**a**hteelo/ta dh**a**hteela*
shoulder	ο ώμος	*o **o**mos*
stomach	το στομάχι	*to stom**a**hee*
throat	ο λαιμός	*o lem**o**s*
tooth/teeth	το δόντι/τα δόντια	*to dh**o**ndee/ta dh**o**ndeea*

car breakdown

you may say ...

Could you please help me?	Μπορείτε να με βοηθήσετε;	*bor**ee**te na me voeeth**ee**sete*
I've broken down.	Το αυτοκίνητό μου χάλασε.	*to aftok**ee**neet**o** moo h**a**lase*
on the Athens-Thessaloniki motorway	στην εθνική οδό Αθήνας-Θεσσαλονίκης	*steen ethneek**ee** odh**o** Ath**ee**nas thesalon**ee**kees*
two kilometres from ...	δύο χιλιόμετρα από ...	*dh**ee**o heeli**o**metra ap**o***

Emergencies

... isn't working. The engine The steering	... δεν δουλεύει. Η μηχανή Το τιμόνι	*... dhen dhoolevee* *ee meehanee* *to teemonee*
The brakes aren't working.	Τα φρένα δεν δουλεύουν.	*ta frena dhen dhoolevoon*
I've got a flat tyre.	Έμεινα από λάστιχο.	*emeena apo lasteeho*
I've run out of petrol.	Έμεινα από βενζίνη.	*emeena apo venzeenee*
When will it be ready?	Πότε θα είναι έτοιμο;	*pote tha eene eteemo*

you may hear ...

Πού βρίσκεστε;	*poo vreeskeste*	Where are you?
Τι βλάβη έχει;	*tee vlavee ehee*	What's the problem?
Θα στείλουμε έναν τεχνίτη αμέσως.	*tha steeloome enan tehneetee amesos*	We'll send a mechanic straight away.
Ποιος είναι ο αριθμός του αυτοκινήτου σας;	*peeos eene o areethmos too aftokeeneetoo sas*	What is your car registration?
Θα είναι έτοιμο ... σε μία ώρα. τη Δευτέρα.	*tha eene eteemo* *se meea ora* *tee deftera*	It will be ready ... in an hour. on Monday.

car parts

accelerator	το γκάζι	*to g**a**zee*
battery	η μπαταρία	*ee batar**ee**a*
brakes	τα φρένα	*ta fr**e**na*
clutch	το χειρόφρενο	*to heer**o**freno*
engine	η μηχανή	*ee meehan**ee***
gears	οι ταχύτητες	*ee tah**ee**teetes*
lights	τα φώτα	*ta f**o**ta*
radiator	το ψυγείο	*to pseey**ee**o*
steering wheel	το τιμόνι	*to teem**o**nee*
tyres	τα λάστιχα	*ta l**a**steeha*
wheels	οι ρόδες	*ee r**o**dhes*
windscreen wiper	ο υαλοκαθαριστήρας	*o eealokathareest**ee**ras*

check out 2

Your hire car has broken down, so you call a mechanic from an emergency phone.

❍ Το αυτοκίνητό μου χάλασε.
*to aftokeen**ee**to moo h**a**lase*

- Πού είσαστε;
*poo **ee**saste*

❍ Στην Εθνική Οδό Αθήνας-Θεσσαλονίκης.
*steen ethneek**ee** odh**o** Ath**ee**nas Thessalon**ee**kees*

- Ερχόμαστε.
*erh**o**maste*

❍ Πόση ώρα θα κάνετε;
*p**o**see **o**ra tha k**a**nete*

- Μισή ώρα.
*mees**ee** ora*

(ερχόμαστε = we're coming)

Q It will take them an hour to come to your rescue: true or false?

at the police station

you may say ...

I've lost my ...	Έχασα ...	**e**hasa
wallet.	το πορτοφόλι μου.	to portof**o**lee moo
passport.	το διαβατήριό μου.	to dheeavat**ee**ree**o** moo
I've had my ... stolen.	Μου έκλεψαν ...	moo **e**klepsan
watch	το ρολόι μου.	to rol**o**ee moo
bag	την τσάντα μου.	teen ts**a**nda moo
Our car has been broken into.	Διέρρηξαν το αυτοκίνητό μας.	dhee**e**reeksan to aftok**ee**neet**o** mas
I was mugged.	Με έκλεψαν.	me **e**klepsan
I've been attacked.	Μου επιτέθηκαν.	moo epeet**e**theekan
yesterday ...	χτες το ...	hthes to
morning	πρωί	pro**ee**
evening	απόγευμα	ap**o**yevma
Just now!	Μόλις τώρα!	m**o**lees t**o**ra
A few minutes ago.	Πριν από λίγο.	preen ap**o** l**ee**gho
in the street	στο δρόμο	sto dhr**o**mo
in a shop	σ' ένα μαγαζί	s**e**na maghaz**ee**
in my hotel	στο ξενοδοχείο μου	sto ksenodhoh**ee**o moo
It's ...	Είναι ...	**ee**ne
blue.	μπλε.	ble
expensive.	ακριβό.	akreev**o**
made of leather.	από δέρμα.	ap**o** dh**e**rma

you may hear ...

Πότε/ Πού συνέβη;	*p**o**te/poo seen**e**vee*	When/Where did it happen?
Τι έγινε;	*tee **e**yeene*	What happened?
Πώς λέγεστε;	*pos l**e**yeste*	What's your name?
Πού μένετε;	*poo m**e**nete*	Where are you staying?
Ποια είναι η διεύθυνσή σας;	*pee**a** **ee**ne ee dheee**e**ftheens**ee** sas*	What's your address?
Συμπληρώστε αυτό το έντυπο.	*seembleer**o**ste aft**o** to **e**ndeepo*	Fill in this form.
Ελάτε αργότερα.	*el**a**te argh**o**tera*	Come back later.

check out 3

You are reporting the loss of your camera at the police station.

- ❍ Έχασα τη φωτογραφική μηχανή μου.
  *ehasa tee fotoghrafeek**ee** meehan**ee** moo*
- \- Πού;
  poo
- ❍ Στο ξενοδοχείο μου.
  *sto ksenodhoh**ee**o moo*
- \- Πού μένετε;
  *poo m**e**nete*
- ❍ Στο ξενοδοχείο Αύρα
  *sto ksenodhoh**ee**o **a**vra*
- \- Συμπληρώστε αυτό το έντυπο.
  *seembleer**o**stee aft**o** to **e**ndeepo*

(ξενοδοχείο = hotel)

Q What are you asked to do?

valuables

briefcase	ο χαρτοφύλακας	*o hartofe**e**lakas*
(digital) camera	η (ψηφιακή) φωτογραφική μηχανή	*ee (pseefeeak**ee**) fotoghrafeek**ee** meehan**ee***
credit card	η πιστωτική κάρτα	*ee peestoteek**ee** k**a**rta*
driving licence	η άδεια οδήγησης	*ee **a**dheea odh**ee**yeesees*
handbag	η τσάντα	*ee ts**a**nda*
jewellery	τα κοσμήματα	*ta kozm**ee**mata*
laptop	το λάπτοπ	*to laptop*
mobile phone	το κινητό τηλέφωνο	*to keeneet**o** teel**e**fono*
money	τα χρήματα	*ta hr**ee**mata*
mp3 player	το mp3 player	*to mp3 pl**e**ee-er*
passport	το διαβατήριο	*to dheeavat**ee**reeo*
purse/wallet	το πορτοφόλι	*to portof**o**lee*
suitcase	η βαλίτσα	*ee val**ee**tsa*
tickets	τα εισιτήρια	*ta eeseet**ee**reea*

sound check

Γ, γ can be pronounced in a number of ways depending on the letter that follows it:

γόνατο *gh**o**nato*

γιατρός *yatr**o**s*

Αγγλικά *angleek**a***

δάγκωσε *dh**a**ngose*

Practise on these words:

για *ya*

αγκώνας *ang**o**nas*

συγνώμη *seeghn**o**mee*

σαγόνι *sagh**o**nee*

try it out

match it up

Match the two halves of the words to make five things you might lose on holiday, e.g. τσά + ντα = τσάντα, bag.

χρή	φόλι
βαλί	τήριο
πορτο	ματα
διαβα	τσα
κοσμή	ματα

as if you were there

You've burned yourself sunbathing, and go to the chemist's for help. Follow the prompts to play your part.

(Say good morning)
Καλημέρα.
(Ask if they have something for sunburn)
Βάλτε αυτή την κρέμα τρεις φορές την ημέρα.
(Ask if they have after-sun lotion)
Ορίστε.
(Ask how much it is altogether)

linkup

Πού είναι το πιο κοντινό νοσοκομείο; *poo **ee**ne to pee**o** kondeen**o** nosokom**ee**o*	**Where is the nearest** hospital?
Χρειάζομαι γιατρό. *hree**a**zome yatro*	**I need** a doctor.
Έχω διάρροια. *__e__ho dee**a**reea*	**I have** diarrhoea.
Έχω δυσκοιλιότητα. *__e__ho dheeskeelee**o**teeta*	**I am** constipated.
Πονάει το στομάχι μου. *pon**a**ee to stom**a**hee moo*	My stomach **hurts**.
Έχασα το διαβατήριό μου. *__e__hasa to dheeavat**ee**ree**o** moo*	**I've lost** my passport.

saying what's wrong

There are two simple ways of saying what's hurting:

Πονάει το στομάχι μου. My stomach **hurts**.
*pon**a**ee to stom**a**hee moo*

Έχω ένα πόνο στο στομάχι μου. **I have a pain** in my stomach.
*__e__ho __e__na p**o**no sto stom**a**hee moo*

Some common ailments have a special phrase:

Έχω πονοκέφαλο. *__e__ho ponok**e**falo* I have a headache.

possession

To say 'my' in Greek, you use 'the ... of me', so 'my shoulder' is ο ώμος μου *o **o**mos moo* (literally, the shoulder of me).

For 'your, his, her' etc. see the Language Builder p138.

Using the words and phrases in this book will enable you to deal with most everyday situations. If you want to go a bit further and start building your own phrases, there are a few rules about Greek that will help you.

gender

All nouns (words for people, things, places, concepts, names) in Greek are masculine, feminine or neuter. As you go along you'll probably recognise that most words ending in **-ος**, **-ας** or **-ης** are masculine, those ending in **-α** or **-η** are feminine and those ending in **-ο** or **-ι** are neuter. Words 'borrowed' from English, such as σουπερμάρκετ *soopermarket* (supermarket) are also neuter.

words for 'a' and 'the'

The gender (masculine, feminine or neuter) of a word affects the form of 'a' and 'the' used with it.

	a/an	the – singular	the – plural
masculine	ένας *enas*	ο *o*	οι *ee*
feminine	μία *meea*	η *ee*	οι *ee*
neuter	ένα *ena*	το *to*	τα *ta*

Some examples of 'a/an':
ένας δρόμος *enas dhromos* a road
μία εφημερίδα *meea efeemereedha* a newspaper
ένα περιοδικό *ena pereeodheeko* a magazine

With plurals, there is no word in Greek for 'some' or 'any':
Θέλω μπανάνες *thelo bananes* I want some bananas
Έχετε παιδιά; *ehete pedheea* Do you have any children?

Some examples of 'the':
ο όροφος *o orofos* the floor
οι όροφοι *ee orofee* the floors

η φούστα *ee foosta* the skirt
οι φούστες *ee foostes* the skirts
το δωμάτιο *to dhomateeo* the room
τα δωμάτια *ta dhomateea* the rooms

As you may have noticed there are certain expressions where Greek uses 'the' and English doesn't. The main instances are:

- with place names and other 'proper' nouns:
  Είμαι από το Λονδίνο. *eeme apo to londheeno* I'm from London.
  Ο Κώστας είναι Έλληνας. *o kostas eene eleenas* Kostas is Greek.
- when talking about what's yours, his, ours (see p138)
- when talking about what you like and don't like (see p139)

singular & plural

When you talk about more than one person or thing, the ending of the noun changes, and there are certain patterns which will help you make the correct changes:

masculine words
-ος changes to **-οι**
ένας σάκος *enas sakos* a/one bag
δύο σάκοι *dheeo sakee* two bags

-ης changes to **-ες**
ένας χάρτης *enas hartees* a/one map
δύο χάρτες *dheeo hartes* two maps

-ας changes to **-ες**
ένας άντρας *enas andras* a/one man
δύο άντρες *dheeo andres* two men

feminine words
-α changes to **-ες**
μία μπύρα *meea beera* a/one beer
δύο μπύρες *dheeo beeres* two beers

-η changes to **-ες**
μία κόρη *meea koree* a/one daughter
δύο κόρες *dheeo kores* two daughters

neuter words
-ο changes to **-α**
ένα τσιγάρο *ena tseegharo* a/one cigarette
δύο τσιγάρα *dheeo tseeghara* two cigarettes

-ι changes to **-ια**
ένα πεπόνι *ena peponee* a/one melon
δύο πεπόνια *dheeo peponeea* two melons

Words 'borrowed' from English don't change:
ένα σουπερμάρκετ *ena soopermarket* a/one supermarket

note masculine nouns and names all end in **-ς** (s):
Πέτρος *petros* Peter
μουσακάς *moosakas* moussaka
χάρτης *hartees* map
However, the **ς** is often left off for various reasons. For example, if you are addressing your friend Petros, you'd say Πέτρο! *petro*, Andreas would be Ανδρέα! *andrea* and so on.

Also, if you're asking for something masculine, such as a map or a moussaka, you'd say:
Έχετε ένα χάρτη της πόλης; *ehete ena hartee tees polees*
Have you got a map of the town?
'Ενα μουσακά παρακαλώ *ena moosaka parakalo*
A/One moussaka please.
(Note that the word ένας *enas* meaning 'a/one' also loses its ς here.) This only happens for masculine nouns.

adjectives

The endings of adjectives change depending on whether they refer to a masculine, feminine or neuter, singular or plural word

The most common adjective endings are:
singular masculine **-ος** *os*; feminine **-η** *ee*; neuter **-o** *o*
plural masculine **-οι** *ee*; feminine **-ες** *es*; neuter **-α** *a*

So for a word like 'small', it would be:
singular masculine μικρός *meekr**o**s*; feminine μικρή *meekr**ee***; neuter μικρό *meekr**o***
plural masculine μικροί *meekr**ee***; feminine μικρές *meekr**e**s*; neuter μικρά *meekr**a***

Some more examples:
ο στενός δρόμος *o sten**o**s dhr**o**mos* the narrow road
η μικρή εκκλησία *ee meekr**ee** ekleese**e**a* the small church
το μεγάλο μουσείο *to megh**a**lo moos**ee**o* the large museum

οι στενοί δρόμοι *ee sten**ee** dhr**o**mee* the narrow roads
η μικρές εκκλησίες *ee meekr**e**s eklees**ee**es* the small churches
τα μεγάλα μουσεία *ta megh**a**la moos**ee**a* the large museums

verbs

Verbs (words for doing or being) change their endings in Greek depending on:
- who or what is doing the action (the 'subject')
- how many subjects there are (singular/plural)
- when something is done (i.e. in the present, past or future)

Πόσο κάνει το πεπόνι; *p**o**so k**a**nee to pep**o**nee*
How much does the melon ('it') cost?
Πόσο κάνουν τα πεπόνια; *p**o**so k**a**noon ta pep**o**neea*
How much do the melons ('they') cost?
Μιλάω Ελληνικά. *meel**a**o eleeneek**a***
I speak Greek.
Η κόρη μου μιλάει Ελληνικά. *ee k**o**ree moo meel**a**ee eleeneek**a***
My daughter speaks Greek.

There are patterns you can learn, which will help you choose the right ending. In the chart below, you can see the whole present tense of the verb θέλω *th**e**lo* (to want), which shows the endings of the most common group of verbs.

θέλω: to want		
θέλ**ω**	*th**e**lo*	I want
θέλ**εις**	*th**e**lees*	you want (singular informal)
θέλ**ει**	*th**e**lee*	he/she/it wants
θέλ**ουμε**	*th**e**loome*	we want
θέλ**ετε**	*th**e**lete*	you want (plural/formal)
θέλ**ουν**	*th**e**loon*	they want

Some verbs don't follow this regular pattern and have to be learnt separately, as the verb είμαι ***ee**me* (to be):

είμαι: to be		
είμαι	***ee**me*	I am
είσαι	***ee**se*	you are (singular informal)
είναι	***ee**ne*	he, she, it is
είμαστε	***ee**maste*	we are
είσαστε/είστε	***ee**saste/**ee**ste*	you are (plural/formal)
είναι	***ee**ne*	they are

In Greek there is no infinitive (to have, to be, to live), so if you want to look up a verb in the dictionary, it will be listed as the first person singular, the 'I' form (I have, I am, I live).

the different words for 'you'

The general rule is that εσείς *es**ee**s* and the verb ending -ετε *ete* are used for speaking to a stranger (formal) or to more than one person and εσύ *es**ee*** and the verb ending -εις *ees* are used for talking to just one person, usually a friend or someone you know (informal). If you're not sure which to use to one person, it's probably better to use εσείς and -ετε when you first meet, especially if they are older.

Language **Builder**

pronouns

In Greek it is not usually necessary to use the word for 'I', 'you', 'he', 'she', 'they', and 'it' (pronouns). This is because they are implied by the verb ending. However, they are used:

- to emphasise the subject:
  Εγώ θέλω τσάι. Τι θέλεις εσύ; *egh**o** th**e**lo ts**a**ee. tee th**e**lees es**ee***
  I want tea. What do you want?
- to distinguish between 'he' and 'she' as this is not always clear because they have the same verb ending:
  Αυτός είναι Έλληνας και αυτή είναι Αγγλίδα. *aft**o**s **ee**ne **e**leenas ke aft**ee** **ee**ne angl**ee**dha* He's Greek and she's English.
- When the pronoun stands on its own, without a verb:
  Τι κάνετε; *tee k**a**nete* How are you?
  Καλά. Εσείς; *kal**a**. es**ee**s* Fine. You?

The chart below shows all of the pronouns, and which form of the verb θέλω *th**e**lo* (to want) they go with:

εγώ	*egh**o***	I	θέλω
εσύ	*es**ee***	you (singular informal)	θέλεις
αυτός	*aft**o**s*	he	θέλει
αυτή	*aft**ee***	she	
αυτό	*aft**o***	it	
εμείς	*em**ee**s*	we	θέλουμε
εσείς	*es**ee**s*	you (plural/formal)	θέλετε
αυτοί	*aft**ee***	they (masculine)	θέλουν
αυτές	*aft**e**s*	they (feminine)	
αυτά	*aft**a***	they (neuter)	

questions

To ask a question which only expects the answer 'yes' or 'no', simply use the sentence you'd use for making a statement and change the intonation of your voice to a rising tone.

Έχετε μήλα. *ehete meela* You have apples.
Έχετε μήλα; *ehete meela* Do you have (any) apples?

You can also use question words, as you would in English. Some of the common ones are:

Πόσο; *poso* How much?
Πότε; *pote* When?
Τι; *tee* What?
Πού; *poo* Where?
Πώς; *pos* How?

If you're interested in reading or writing Greek, don't forget the Greek question mark is like our semicolon **;**
e.g. Πόσο θέλετε; *poso thelete* How much do you want?

negatives

If you want to make a 'negative' statement, simply put the word δεν *dhen* (not) before the verb; there is no need for 'doesn't' and 'don't' as in English:
Δεν έχω μήλα. *then eho meela* I don't have any apples
Δεν θέλει κρασί; *then thelee krasee* Doesn't he want (any) wine?

talking about possession

To talk about 'my', 'your', etc., use the following words, positioned after the noun:
my μου *moo*
your σου *soo* (singular informal)
your σας *sas* (plural/formal)
his του *too*
her της *tees*
its του *too*
our μας *mas*
their τους *toos*
Remember you need to use the appropriate word for 'the'

before the person or item you're naming:
ο άντρας μου *o **a**ndras moo* my husband
οι γονείς μας *ee ghon**ee**s mas* our parents
τα βιβλία τους *ta veevl**ee**a toos* their books

talking about likes & dislikes

The way you say what you like in Greek is very different from the English.
Μ' αρέσει. *mar**e**see* I like it. (literally, it pleases me)
Μ' αρέσουν. *mar**e**soon* I like them. (literally, they please me)

Remember you need to use the appropriate word for 'the' before the person or item you're naming:

Μ' αρέσει το κόκκινο κρασί, δεν μ' αρέσει η μπύρα. *mar**e**see to k**o**keeno kras**ee** dhen mar**e**see ee b**ee**ra*
I like red wine, I don't like beer.

Μ' αρέσουν οι μελιτζάνες, δεν μ' αρέσουν τα καρότα. *mar**e**soon ee meleeds**a**nes dhen mar**e**soon ta kar**o**ta*
I like aubergines, I don't like carrots.

What you are literally saying is 'the red wine pleases me'; 'the aubergines please me'.

Μ' αρέσει is short for μου αρέσει *moo ar**e**see*. If you want to talk about what other people like or don't like, use the same words as for 'my' 'your' etc. (See 'talking about possession' on the previous page.)
Δεν μας αρέσει το ούζο. *dhen mas ar**e**see to **oo**zo* We don't like ouzo.
Τους αρέσουν οι ελιές; *toos ar**e**soon ee el**ee**es* Do they like olives?

Answers

Bare Necessities.......

check out

1 left
2 oranges
3 on business; two
4 145; your passport

question time

1c 2a 3e 4d 5b

as if you were there

Γεια σου. Πολύ καλά, ευχαριστώ.
*ya soo. pol**ee** kal**a** efhareest**o***
Με λένε Σάρα.
*me l**e**ne s**a**ra*
Είμαι από τη Σκωτία. Είμαι από το Εδιμβούργο.
***ee**me ap**o** tee skot**ee**a. **ee**me ap**o** to edheemv**oo**rgo*

Getting Around.........

check out

1 false, the station is on the left
2 true
3 at 8 o' clock in the morning; at 2 o'clock
4 false, you were asked whether you wanted single or return; €60

mind the gap

μικρό, ευχαριστώ, τι, ρέστα, ορίστε
new word: μετρό

as if you were there

Τι ώρα φεύγει το τρένο για τον Πύργο; *tee **o**ra f**e**vyee to tr**e**no ya ton p**ee**rgho*
Πόση ώρα κάνει;
*p**o**see **o**ra k**a**nee*
Πρέπει ν' αλλάξω;
*pr**e**pee nal**a**kso*
Δύο με επιστροφή
*dh**ee**o me epeestrof**ee***

Somewhere to Stay.....

check out

1 €20; no
2 true; room 230
3 at 6 o'clock; false, from 7.30 to 10.30am
4 Loutra

match it up

1f 2c 3e 4a 5d 6b

in the mix

Καλημέρα σας.
*kaleem**e**ra sas*
Έχω κλείσει ένα μονόκλινο.
*e**h**o kl**ee**see **e**na mon**o**kleeno*
Το όνομά σας παρακαλώ.
*to **o**nom**a** sas parakal**o***
Τζον Σμιθ.
john smith
Το διαβατήριό σας παρακαλώ.
*to dheeavat**ee**ree**o** sas parakal**o***
Ορίστε!
*or**ee**ste*
Συμπληρώστε αυτό το έντυπο.
*seembleer**o**ste aft**o** to **e**ndeepo*

as if you were there

Καλημέρα, έχετε δίκλινο δωμάτιο;
*kaleem**e**ra **e**hete dh**ee**kleeno dhom**a**teeo*

Ναι, πόσο κοστίζει τη βραδιά;
*ne p**o**so kost**ee**zee tee vradhee**a***
Δύο βραδιές.
*dh**ee**o vradh**ee**es*

Ορίστε.
*or**ee**ste*
Παρακαλώ, γεια σας.
*parakal**o** ya sas*

Buying Things..........

check out

1 false
2 €12.30
3 false, you asked for 100g
4 no, only blue and brown

mind the gap

1 τυρί
2 γιαούρτι
3 ζαμπόν
4 ψωμί
5 πεπόνι
6 ντομάτα

money talk

total: €5,60

as if you were there

Ένα τέταρτο τυρί.
*e**na** te**tarto teer**ee***
Διακόσια γραμμάρια ζαμπόν και ταραμοσαλάτα.
*dheeak**o**seea ghram**a**reea zamb**o**n ke taramosal**a**ta*
Λίγο ακόμα.
*l**ee**gho ak**o**ma*
Τρία λεμόνια και μία σοκολάτα παρακαλώ. Αυτά, ευχαριστώ.
*tr**ee**a lem**o**neea ke m**ee**a sokol**a**ta parakal**o**. aft**a** efhareest**o***

Café Life.................

check out

1 a ham and cheese sandwich
2 €12
3 no; false, you order chocolate ice cream

order, order

a φραπέ, γρανίτα, χυμό πορτοκάλι
b καφές, τσάι, καπουτσίνο, ροφήματα
c ούζο, κρασί κόκκινο, τζιν, μπύρα

as if you were there

Τι γλυκά έχετε;
*tee ghleek**a** **e**hete*
Έχετε γρανίτα;
***e**hete ghran**ee**ta*
Μία σοκολατίνα και μία πορτοκαλάδα, παρακαλώ.
*m**ee**a sokolat**ee**na ke m**ee**a portokal**a**dha parakal**o***

Eating Out..............

check out

1 four; false, they are full
2 no; baked, stuffed aubergines
3 Retsina

mind the gap

1d 2c 3e 4f 5a 6b

as if you were there

Καλησπέρα. Μία ταραμοσαλάτα και μία μερίδα πατάτες τηγανητές.
kaleespera. meea taramosalata ke meea mereedha patates teeghaneetes
Μία φέτα και μία σαλάτα, παρακαλώ.
meea feta ke meea salata parakalo
Ένα μπουκάλι κόκκινο κρασί.
ena bookalee kokeeno krasee
Ένα μπουκάλι άσπρο κρασί.
ena bookalee aspro krasee

Entertainment..........

check out

1 midday
2 Wednesday; false, you buy tickets
3 4 and 6 o'clock

in the mix

1 πινακοθήκη
2 θέατρο
3 παραλία
4 πισίνα
5 κλαμπ

as if you were there

Τι ώρα ανοίγει το κλαμπ;
tee ora aneeyee to klab
Τι ώρα αρχίζει το πρόγραμμα;
tee ora arheezee to proghrama
Χρειάζονται εισιτήρια;
hreeazonde eeseeteereea
Ευχαριστώ.
efhareesto

Emergencies............

check out

1 three times a day; false, before meals
2 false, half an hour
3 fill in a form

match it up

χρήματα money
βαλίτσα suitcase
πορτοφόλι wallet
διαβατήριο passport
κοσμήματα jewellery

as if you were there

Καλημέρα.
kaleemera
Έχετε κάτι για έγκαυμα από τον ήλιο;
ehete katee ya engavma apo ton eeleeo
Έχετε γαλάκτωμα για μετά τον ήλιο;
ehete ghalaktoma ya meta ton eeleeo
Πόσο κάνουν όλα μαζί;
poso kanoon ola mazee

(m) = masculine (f) = feminine
(n) = neuter (p) = plural
Note that Greek has no infinitives, so the 'I' form of the verb is given.

A

a, an/one ένας/ένα (m, n) *enas/ena*
a, an/one (fem) μία (f) *meea*
adaptor μετασχηματιστής (m) *metas-heemateestees*
address διεύθυνση (f) *dheeeftheensee*
adult μεγάλος, η, -ο *meghalos-ee-o*
aeroplane αεροπλάνο (n) *aeroplano*
to ache/hurt πονάω *ponao*
after-sun lotion γαλάκτωμα για μετά τον ήλιο (n) *ghalaktoma ya meta ton eeleeo*
air αέρας (m) *aeras*
air conditioning ερ κοντίσιον (n) *er condeeseeon*
airport αεροδρόμιο (n) *aerodhromeeo*
alabaster αλάβαστρο (n) *alavastro*
allergic αλλεργικός, -η, -ο *aleryeekos-ee-o*
alone ήσυχος, -η, -ο *eeseehos-ee-o*
leave me alone άσε με ήσυχο *ase me eeseeho*
altogether όλα μαζί *ola mazee*
ambulance ασθενοφόρο (n) *asthenoforo*
and και *ke*
ankle αστράγαλος (m) *astraghalos*
antibiotics αντιβιοτικό (n) *andeeveeoteeko*
antihistamine αντιισταμινικό (n) *andee-eestameeneeko*
antiquities αρχαιότητες (f, pl) *arheoteetes*
anyone κάποιος, -α, -ο *kapeeos-a-o*
anything else τίποτ' άλλο *teepot alo*
apartment διαμέρισμα (n) *dheeamereesma*
apple μήλο (n) *meelo*
apricot βερίκοκο (n) *vereekoko*
armbands μπρατσάκια (npl) *bratsakeea*
arrival άφιξη (f) *afeeksee*
to arrive φτάνω *ftano*
as far as/until μέχρι *mehree*
aspirin ασπιρίνη (f) *aspeereenee*
at, to, on, in the στον (m) στην (f) στο (n) *ston steen sto*
aubergine μελιτζάνα (f) *meleedsana*

B

baby food βρεφική τροφή (f) *vrefeekee trofee*
back πλάτη (f) *platee*
backgammon τάβλι (n) *tavlee*
bag τσάντα (f) *tsanda*
bakery φούρνος (m) *foornos*
balcony μπαλκόνι (n) *balkonee*
ball μπάλα (f) *bala*
banana μπανάνα (f) *banana*
bar μπαρ (n) *bar*
basement υπόγειο (n) *eepoyeeo*
basketball μπάσκετ (n) *basket*
bathroom μπάνιο (n) *baneeo*
battery μπαταρία (f) *batareea*
beach παραλία (f) *paraleea*
to be είμαι *eeme*
bed, lounger κρεβάτι (n) *krevatee*
beer μπύρα (f) *beera*
to begin αρχίζω *arheezo*
beige μπεζ *bez*
belt ζώνη (f) *zonee*
big μεγάλος, -η, -ο *meghalos-ee-o*
bike ποδήλατο (n) *podheelato*
bill λογαριασμός (m) *loghareeazmos*
biscuit μπισκότο (n) *beeskoto*
a bit λίγο *leegho*
to bite δαγκώνω *dhangono*
black μαύρος, -η, -ο *mavros-ee-o*
blanket κουβέρτα (f) *kooverta*
blind ρολό (n) *rolo*
blue μπλε *ble*
boat σκάφος (n) *skafos*
bone κόκαλο (n) *kokalo*
book βιβλίο (n) *veevleeo*
bookshop βιβλιοπωλείο (n) *veevleeopoleeo*
boot μπότα (f) *bota*
bottle μπουκάλι (n) *bookalee*
bowl μπολ (n) *bol*
bread ψωμί (n) *psomee*
to break (limb) σπάω *spao*
to break down (car) παθαίνω βλάβη *patheno vlavee*
breakfast πρωινό (n) *proeeno*
to breathe αναπνέω *anapneo*
bridge γέφυρα (f) *gefeera*

briefcase χαρτοφύλακας (m) *hartofeelakas*
to bring φέρνω *ferno*
brown καφέ *kafe*
to burn καίω *keo*
bus λεωφορείο (n) *leoforeeo*
bus stop στάση (f) *stasee*
butcher κρεοπωλείο (n) *kreopoleeo*
to buy αγοράζω *aghorazo*

C

cabbage λάχανο (n) *lahano*
cabin καμπίνα (f) *kabeena*
to call καλώ *kalo*
to call (phone) τηλεφωνώ *teelefono*
camera (φωτογραφική) μηχανή (f) *(fotoghrafeekee) meehanee*
campsite κάμπιγκ (n) *campeeng*
can (to be able) μπορώ *boro*
car αυτοκίνητο (n) *aftokeeneeto*
car park πάρκινγκ (n) *parkeeng*
caravan τροχόσπιτο (n) *trohospeeto*
carpet χαλί (n) *halee*
carrots καρότα (n) *karota*
cash μετρητά (n) *metreeta*
castle κάστρο (n) *kastro*
cathedral μητρόπολη (f) *meetropolee*
central heating καλοριφέρ (n) *kaloreefer*
central/main κεντρικός, -η, -ο *kendreekos-ee-o*
centre κέντρο (n) *kendro*
cents (euro) λεπτά (n) *lepta*
ceramics κεραμικά (n) *kerameeka*
certainly/of course μάλιστα *maleesta*
to change αλλάζω *alazo*
change (coins) ρέστα (n) *resta*
changing rooms αποδυτήρια (n) *apodheeteereea*
cheaper φθηνότερο *ftheenotero*
to check ελέγχω *elenho*
cheese τυρί (n) *teeree*
chemist's φαρμακείο (n) *farmakeeo*
cherry κεράσι (n) *kerasee*
chest στήθος (n) *steethos*
chewing gum τσίχλα (f) *tseehla*
chicken κοτόπουλο (n) *kotopoolo*
child παιδί (n) *pedhee*
for a child παιδικός, -η, -ο *pedheekos-ee-o*
chocolate σοκολάτα (f) *sokolata*
chop (of meat) μπριζόλα (f) *breezola*
church εκκλησία (f) *ekleeseea*
cigarettes τσιγάρα (n) *tseeghara*
cinema σινεμά (n) *seenema*
class θέση (f) *thesee*
climbing ορειβασία (f) *oreevaseea*
cloakroom βεστιάριο (n) *vesteeareeo*
close κοντινός, -η, -ο *kondeenos-ee-o*
clothes ρούχα (n) *rooha*
clothes shop κατάστημα ενδυμάτων (n) *katasteema endheematon*
coffee καφές (m) *kafes*
cold κρύος, -α, -ο *kreeos-a-o*
colour χρώμα (n) *hroma*
concert συναυλία (f) *seenavleea*
concession έκπτωση (f) *ekptosee*
condom προφυλακτικό (n) *profeelakteeko*
to connect συνδέω/συνδέομαι *seendheo/seendheome*
constipation δυσκοιλιότητα (f) *dheeskeeleeoteeta*
contact lens solution υγρό φακών επαφής (n) *eeghro fakon epafees*
contact lenses φακοί επαφής (m) *fakee epafees*
to contain περιέχω *pereeeho*
to cook ψήνω *pseeno*
cookie κουλουράκι (n) *kooloorakee*
to cost κοστίζω *kosteezo*
cotton (fabric) βαμβακερό *vamvakero*
couchette κουκέτα (f) *kooketa*
cough mixture σιρόπι για το βήχα *seeropee ya to veeha*
courgette κολοκυθάκι (n) *kolokeethakee*
cream κρέμα (f) *krema*
credit card πιστωτική κάρτα (f) *peestoteekee karta*
cucumber αγγουράκι (n) *angoorakee*
cup φλυτζάνι (n) *fleedsanee*
to cut κόβω *kovo*

D

dairy shop γαλακτοπωλείο (n) *ghalaktopoleeo*
dark σκούρος, -η, -ο *skooros-ee-o*
daughter κόρη (f) *koree*
day ημέρα (f)/μέρα (f) *eemera/mera*
deckchair ξαπλώστρα (f) *ksaplostra*
delicious νοστιμότατος *nosteemotatos*

dentist οδοντίατρος (m/f) *odhondeeatros*
deodorant αποσμητικό (n) *apozmeeteeko*
department τμήμα (n) *tmeema*
department store πολυκατάστημα (n) *poleekatasteema*
departure αναχώρηση (f) *anahoreesee*
dessert επιδόρπιο (n) *epeedhorpeeo*
to develop εμφανίζω *emfaneezo*
diabetic διαβητικός, -η, -ο *dheeaveeteekos-ee-o*
to dial παίρνω *perno*
diarrhoea διάρροια (f) *deeareea*
diesel ντίζελ (n) *deezel*
digital camera ψηφιακή μηχανή (f) *pseefeeakee meehanee*
dinghy (rubber) λαστιχένια βάρκα (f) *lasteeheneea varka*
disposable μιας χρήσεως *mias hreeseos*
to do κάνω *kano*
doctor γιατρός (m/f) *yatros*
dog σκύλος (m) *skeelos*
door πόρτα (f) *porta*
double (room) δίκλινο (n) *dheekleeno*
double (food portion, drinks measure) διπλός, -η, -ο *dheeplos-ee-o*
dress φόρεμα (n) *forema*
drink ποτό (n) *poto*
to drink πίνω *peeno*
driving license δίπλωμα οδήγησης (n) *dheeploma odheeyeesees*
dustbin σκουπιδοντενεκές (m) *skoopeedhondenekes*

E

ear αυτί (n) *aftee*
eau de cologne κολόνια (f) *koloneea*
egg αυγό (n) *avgho*
elbow αγκώνας (m) *angonas*
end τέλος (n) *telos*
enjoy your meal! καλή όρεξη! *kalee oreksee*
enough αρκετά *arketa*
entertainment διασκέδαση (f) *dheeaskedasee*
euro ευρώ (n) *evro*
even ζυγός, -η, -ο *zeeghos-ee-o*
evening βράδυ (n)/βραδιά *vradhee/vradheea*
excuse me συγνώμη (f) *seeghnomee*
exit έξοδος (f) *eksodhos*
eye μάτι (n) *matee*

F

far (away) μακριά *makreea*
ferry φέρρυ μπόουτ (n) *feree booot*
festival φεστιβάλ (n) *festeeval*
fever πυρετός (m) *peeretos*
fig σύκο (n) *seeko*
to fill in συμπληρώνω *seembleerono*
to fill up γεμίζω *yemeezo*
filling (for tooth) σφράγισμα (n) *sfrayeezma*
film φιλμ (n) *feelm*
finger δάχτυλο (n) *dhahteelo*
to finish τελειώνω *teleeono*
fireworks πυροτεχνήματα (n) *peerotehneemata*
first πρώτος, -η, -ο *protos-ee-o*
fish ψάρι (n) *psaree*
fishmonger's ιχθυοπωλείο/ψαράδικο (n) *eehtheeopoleeo/psaradheeko*
fitness centre γυμναστήριο (n) *yeemnasteereeo*
flight πτήση (f) *pteesee*
flip flops σαγιονάρες (fpl) *sayeeonares*
flippers βατραχοπέδιλα (npl) *vatrahopedheela*
floor όροφος (m) *orofos*
flour αλεύρι (n) *alevree*
Flying Dolphin (catamaran) ιπτάμενο δελφίνι (n) *eeptameno dhelfeenee*
foot πόδι (n) *podhee*
football ποδόσφαιρο (n) *podhosfero*
for για *ya*
fork πιρούνι (n) *peeroonee*
form έντυπο (n) *endeepo*
free ελεύθερος, -η, -ο *eleftheros-ee-o*
fridge ψυγείο (n) *pseeyeeo*
from από *apo*
fruit φρούτο (n) *frooto*
full γεμάτος, -η, -ο *yematos-ee-o*
further on πιο κάτω *peeo kato*

G

gallery πινακοθήκη (f) *peenakoth**ee**kee*
garden κήπος (m) *k**ee**pos*
garlic σκόρδο (n) *sk**o**rdho*
Gents (toilets) ανδρών (m) *andhr**o**n*
to give δίνω *dh**ee**no*
glass ποτήρι (n) *pot**ee**ree*
glossy (photos) γυαλιστερές (φωτογραφίες) *yaleester**e**s fotoghraf**ee**es*
to go πάω *p**a**o*
golf club μπαστούνι του γκολφ (n) *bast**oo**nee too golf*
good καλός, -ή, -ο *kal**o**s-**ee**-**o***
goodbye γεια σας (pl)/γεια σου (sing) *ya sas/ya soo*
good evening καλησπέρα *kaleesp**e**ra*
good morning καλημέρα *kaleem**e**ra*
good night καληνύχτα *kaleen**ee**hta*
gramme γραμμάριο (n) *ghram**a**reeo*
grapefruit γκρέιπ φρουτ (n) *gr**e**eep froot*
grapes σταφύλι (n) *staf**ee**lee*
Greek (language) Ελληνικά (n) *eleeneek**a***
green πράσινος, -η, -ο *pr**a**seenos-ee-o*
green beans φασολάκια (n) *fasol**a**keea*
greengrocer's μανάβικο (n) *man**a**veeko*
grey γκρίζος, -α, -ο *ghr**ee**zos-a-o*
grocer's παντοπωλείο (n) *pandopol**ee**o*
ground floor ισόγειο (n) *ees**o**yeeo*
guesthouse πανσιόν (f) *pansee**o**n*
guide ξεναγός (m, f) *ksenagh**o**s*
guide (book) οδηγός (m) *odheegh**o**s*

H

hairdresser's κομμωτήριο (n) *komot**ee**reeo*
hairdryer πιστολάκι (n)/σεσουάρ (n) *peestol**a**kee/sesoo**a**r*
half μισός *mees**o**s*
half board ημιδιατροφή (f) *eemeedeeatrof**ee***
half price μισοτιμής *meesoteem**ee**s*
ham ζαμπόν (n) *zamb**o**n*
hand χέρι (n) *h**e**ree*
hand cream κρέμα χεριών (f) *kr**e**ma heree**o**n*
to happen συμβαίνει *seemv**e**nee*
hat καπέλο (n) *kap**e**lo*
to have έχω *e**ho*
do you have? έχετε? *e**hete*
to have to πρέπει *pr**e**pee*
hayfever αλλεργικό συνάχι (n) *alergeek**o** seen**a**hee*
head κεφάλι (n) *kef**a**lee*
headache πονοκέφαλος (m) *ponok**e**falos*
heart καρδιά (f) *kardhee**a***
hello γεια σου (sing)/γεια σας (pl) *ya soo/ya sas*
help βοήθεια *vo**ee**theea*
to help βοηθώ *voeeth**o***
here εδώ *edh**o***
here (you are/it is) ορίστε *or**ee**ste*
hip γοφός (m) *gof**o**s*
honey μέλι (n) *m**e**lee*
hospital νοσοκομείο (n) *nosokom**ee**o*
hot ζεστός, -η, -ο *zest**o**s-**ee**-**o***
hotel ξενοδοχείο (n) *ksenodhoh**ee**o*
hour/time ώρα ***o**ra*
how πώς *p**o**s*
how are you? τι κάνεις;/τι κάνετε; *tee k**a**nees/tee k**a**nete*
how do you like it? πώς σου φαίνεται;/πώς σας φαίνεται; *pos soo f**e**nete/pos sas f**e**nete*
how much πόσο *p**o**so*
how much is it? πόσο έχει; *p**o**so **e**hee*
how much is it? πόσο κάνει; *p**o**so k**a**nee*

I

ice πάγος (m) *p**a**ghos*
ice cream παγωτό (n) *paghot**o***
ill άρρωστος, -η, -ο ***a**rostos-**ee**-**o***
in, on, at, to (f, pl) στις *stees*
to be included περιλαμβάνομαι *pereelamv**a**nome*
information πληροφορία (f) *pleerofor**ee**a*
inner εσωτερικός, -η, -ο *esotereek**o**s-**ee**-**o***
insect έντομο (n) ***e**ndomo*
insurance ασφάλεια (f) *asf**a**leea*
to interest ενδιαφέρω *endheeaf**e**ro*
internet ιντερνέτ (n) ***ee**nternet*
interval διάλειμμα (n) *dhee**a**leema*
iron σίδερο (n) *s**ee**dhero*
islands νησιά (npl) *neesee**a***

J

acket σακάκι (n) *sakakee*
acket (women's) ζακέτα (f) *zaketa*
am μαρμελάδα (f) *marmeladha*
ar βάζο (n) *vazo*
eans τζιν (n) *dseen*
ewellery κόσμημα (n) *kozmeema*
uice χυμός (m) *heemos*

K

:o keep κρατάω *kratao*
<ey κλειδί (n) *kleedhee*
<idney νεφρό (n) *nefro*
<ilo κιλό (n) *keelo*
<iosk περίπτερο (n) *pereeptero*
<nee γόνατο (n) *ghonato*
<nife μαχαίρι (n) *maheree*
:o know ξέρω *ksero*

L

.adies (toilet) γυναικών (f) *yeenekon*
amp λάμπα (f) *lamba*
amp (standard) λαμπατέρ (n) *labater*
aundry πλυντήριο (n) *pleendeereeo*
eather (item) δερμάτινο (n) *dhermateeno*
:o leave αφήνω *afeeno*
:o leave (go away) φεύγω *fevgho*
eft αριστερά *areestera*
eft luggage φύλαξη αποσκευών *feelaksee aposkevon*
emon λεμόνι (n) *lemonee*
emonade λεμονάδα (f) *lemonadha*
ess λιγότερο *leeghotero*
 a bit less πιο λίγο *peeo leegho*
esson μάθημα (n) *matheema*
etter γράμμα (n) *ghrama*
ettuce μαρούλι (n) *maroolee*
ife belt σωσίβιο (n) *soseeveeo*
ift ασανσέρ (n) *asanser*
ight φως (n) *fos*
:o like αρέσω *areso*
 I like ... μου αρέσει ... *moo aresee*
ilo στρώμα θαλάσσης (npl) *stroma thalasees*
itre λίτρο (n) *leetro*
ittle/a little λίγος, -η, -ο *leeghos-ee-o*
iver συκώτι (n) *seekotee*
local ντόπιος *dopeeos*
lock κλειδαριά (f) *kleedhareea*
to look κοιτάζω *keetazo*
 I'm just looking απλά κοιτάω *apla keetao*
to look for ψάχνω *psahno*
to lose χάνω *hano*

M

magazine περιοδικό (n) *pereeodheeko*
main κύριος *keereeos*
map χάρτης (m) *hartees*
market αγορά (f) *aghora*
mask (swimming) μάσκα θαλάσσης (f) *maska thalasees*
matches σπίρτα (n) *speerta*
matt ματ *mat*
it matters πειράζει *peerazee*
it doesn't matter δεν πειράζει *dhen peerazee*
medicine φάρμακο (n) *farmako*
medium μέτριος, -α, -ο *metreeos-a-o*
melon πεπόνι (n) *peponee*
memory card κάρτα μνήμης (f) *karta mneemees*
menu κατάλογος (m) *kataloghos*
menu of the day μενού (n) *menoo*
meter μέτρο (n) *metro*
midday μεσημέρι (n) *meseemeree*
midnight μεσάνυχτα *mesaneehta*
milk γάλα (n) *ghala*
minced beef μοσχαρίσιος κιμάς *mos-hareeseeos keemas*
mine/to me μου *moo*
minute λεπτό (n) *lepto*
mistake λάθος (n) *lathos*
mobile phone κινητό τηλέφωνο *keeneeto teelefono*
money χρήματα (n) *hreemata*
more πιο, περισσότερο *peeo, pereesotero*
 more slowly πιο αργά *peeo argha*
morning πρωί (n) *proee*
mosque τζαμί (n) *tzamee*
mouthwash στοματικό διάλυμα (npl) *stomateeko dheealeema*
to move κινούμαι *keenoome*
museum μουσείο (n) *mooseeo*
mushrooms μανιτάρια (n) *maneetareea*

N

name όνομα (n) *onoma*
my name is λέγομαι *leghome*
what's your name? πώς λέγεστε; *pos leyeste*
napkin πετσέτα (f) *petseta*
nappies πάνες (f) *panes*
near κοντά *konda*
neck λαιμός (m) *lemos*
necklace κολιέ (n) *koleee*
to need χρειάζομαι *hreeazome*
next επόμενο *epomeno*
nice ωραίος, -α, -ο *oreos-a-o*
nightclub κλαμπ (n) *klab*
north βορράς (m) *voras*
nose μύτη (f) *meetee*
not δεν *dhen*
number αριθμός (m) *areethmos*
nurse νοσοκόμος (m)/νοσοκόμα (f) *nosokomos/nosokoma*

O

odd μονός, -ή -ό *monos-ee-o*
oil λάδι (n) *ladhee*
okay εντάξει *endaksee*
okra μπάμιες (fpl) *bameees*
on the right δεξιά *dheksia*
one way απλό εισιτήριο *aplo eeseeteereeo*
onion κρεμμύδι (n) *kremeedhee*
only μόνο *mono*
open ανοιχτός, -η, -ο *aneehtos-ee-o*
operation εγχείρηση (f) *enheereesee*
or ή *ee*
orange πορτοκάλι (n) *portokalee*
orangeade πορτοκαλάδα (f) *portokaladha*
to order παραγγέλνω *parangelno*
oregano ρίγανη (f) *reeghanee*
other άλλος, -η, -ο *alos-ee-o*
outer εξωτερικός, -η, -ο *eksotereekos-ee-o*
outside number εξωτερική γραμμή *eksotereekee ghramee*
overcoat παλτό (n) *palto*

P

pancake κρέπα (f) *krepa*
paper χαρτί (n) *hartee*
to park παρκάρω *parkaro*
park πάρκο (n) *parko*
parking στάθμευση (f) *stathmefsee*
to pass by περνάω *pernao*
passport διαβατήριο (n) *dheeavateereeo*
pasta ζυμαρικά (n, pl) *zeemareeka*
pastry πάστα (f) *pasta*
to pay πληρώνω *pleerono*
peach ροδάκινο (n) *rodhakeeno*
pear αχλάδι (n) *ahladee*
peas αρακάς (m) *arakas*
pedestrian zone πεζόδρομος (m) *pezodhromos*
pen στυλό (n) *steelo*
pensioner συνταξιούχος (m/f) *seendakseeoohos*
pepper (spice) πιπέρι (n) *peeperee*
pepper (vegetable) πιπεριά (f) *peepereea*
person άτομο (n) *atomo*
photograph φωτογραφία (f) *fotoghrafeea*
pill χάπι (n) *hapee*
pillow μαξιλάρι (n) *makseelaree*
pink ροζ *roz*
plan σχέδιο (n) *shedheeo*
plane αεροπλάνο (n) *aeroplano*
plasters χανζαπλάστ (n) *hanzaplast*
plate/course πιάτο (n) *peeato*
platform αποβάθρα (f) *apovathra*
to play παίζω *pezo*
play (theatre) θεατρικό έργο (n) *theatreeko e rgho*
please παρακαλώ *parakalo*
pleased to meet you χαίρω πολύ *hero polee*
pocket πακέτο (n) *paketo*
police αστυνομία (f) *asteenomeea*
police station αστυνομικό τμήμα (n) *asteenomeeko tmeema*
port λιμάνι (n) *leemanee*
postcard κάρτα (f) *karta*
potato πατάτα (f) *patata*
pound λίρα (f) *leera*
prescription συνταγή (f) *seendayee*
priority προτεραιότητα (f) *protereoteeta*
problem πρόβλημα (n) *provleema*
programme πρόγραμμα (n) *proghrama*
to put βάζω *vazo*

R

race course ιππόδρομος (m) *eepodrhomos*
racket ρακέτα (f) *raketa*
radiator καλοριφέρ (n) *kaloreefer*
raw άψητος, -η, -ο *apseetos-ee-o*
ready έτοιμος, -η, -ο *eteemos-ee-o*
receipt απόδειξη (f) *apodheeksee*
to recommend συστήνω *seesteeno*
red κόκκινος, -η, -ο *kokeeno-ee-o*
registration number αριθμός κυκλοφορίας *areethmos keekloforeeas*
regular κανονικός, -η, -ο *kanoneekos-ee-o*
to rent νοικιάζω *neekeeazo*
to repeat επαναλαμβάνω *epanalamvano*
to reserve/close κλείνω *kleeno*
restaurant εστιατόριο (n) *esteeatoreeo*
return επιστροφή (f) *epeestrofee*
rocket ρόκα (f) *roka*
room αίθουσα (f) *ethoosa*
room (in hotel) δωμάτιο (n) *dhomateeo*
room service ρουμ σέρβις (n) *room servees*

S

sachet σακουλάκι (n) *sakoolakee*
safe (box) θυρίδα (f) *theereedha*
sailing ιστιοπλοΐα (f) *eesteeoploeea*
sailboat/dinghy καΐκι (n) *kaeekee*
salad σαλάτα (f) *salata*
salt αλάτι (n) *alatee*
same ίδιος, -α, -ο *eedheeos-a-o*
sandals πέδιλα (n) *pedheela*
sandwich σάντουιτς (n) *sandooeets*
sanitary towels σερβιέτες (fpl) *serveeetes*
saucer πιατάκι (n) *peeatakee*
sauna σάουνα (f) *saoona*
scarf μαντήλι (n) *mandeelee*
second δεύτερος, -η, -ο *defteros-ee-o*
to see βλέπω *vlepo*
self-service σελφ σέρβις (n) *self servees*
to send στέλνω *stelno*
serious σοβαρός, -η, -ο *sovaros-ee-o*
shall/will θα *tha*
shampoo σαμπουάν (n) *sampooan*
sheet σεντόνι (n) *sendonee*
ship καράβι (n) *karavee*
shirt πουκάμισο (n) *pookameeso*
shoe παπούτσι (n) *papootsee*
shop μαγαζί (n) *maghazee*
shopping centre εμπορικό κέντρο *emboreeko kendro*
shorts σορτς (n) *sorts*
shoulder ώμος (m) *omos*
to show δείχνω *deehno*
shower ντους (n) *doos*
shutter παντζούρι (n) *padsooree*
to sign υπογράφω *eepoghrafo*
silk μεταξωτό *metaksoto*
silverware ασημικά (n) *aseemeeka*
single room μονόκλινο (n) *monokleeno*
size/number νούμερο (n) *noomero*
skiing σκι (n) *skee*
skirt φούστα (f) *foosta*
slice/type of cheese φέτα (f) *feta*
small μικρός, -η, -ο *meekros-ee-o*
smaller μικρότερος, -η, -ο *meekroteros-ee-o*
to smoke καπνίζω *kapneezo*
snacks πρόχειρο φαγητό (n) *proheero fayeeto*
snorkel αναπνευστήρας (m) *anapnefsteeras*
soap σαπούνι (n) *sapoonee*
socks κάλτσες (f) *kaltses*
soft drink αναψυκτικό (n) *anapseekteeko*
someone κάποιος, -α, -ο *kapeeos-a-o*
something/anything κάτι *katee*
somewhere κάπου *kapoo*
son γιος (m) *yos*
song τραγούδι (n) *traghoodhee*
south νότος (m) *notos*
sparkling ανθρακούχο, με ανθρακικό *anthrakooho, me anthrakeeko*
to speak μιλάω *meelao*
speciality σπεσιαλιτέ (f) *speseealeete*
spinach σπανάκι (n) *spanakee*
spoon κουτάλι (n) *kootalee*
square πλατεία (f) *plateea*

stadium γήπεδο/στάδιο (n) *yeepedo/stadheeo*
stairs σκάλα (f) *skala*
stamp γραμματόσημο (n) *ghramatoseemo*
station (bus, train) σταθμός (m) *stathmos*
to stay μένω *meno*
steering wheel τιμόνι (n) *teemonee*
still (non-sparkling) χωρίς ανθρακικό *horees anthrakeeko*
to sting τσιμπάω *tseembao*
sting τσίμπημα (n) *tseembeema*
stomach στομάχι (n) *stomahee*
straight ίσια *eeseea*
straight on ευθεία (f) *eftheea*
strawberry φράουλα (f) *fraoola*
street δρόμος (m) *dhromos*
students φοιτητές (m) *feeteetees*
stuffed γεμιστά (n) *yemeesta*
subtitle υπότιτλος (m) *eepoteetlos*
sugar ζάχαρη (f) *zaharee*
suitcase βαλίτσα (f) *valeetsa*
sun ήλιος (m) *eeleeos*
sunglasses γυαλιά ηλίου (n) *yaleea eeleeoo*
supermarket σουπερμάρκετ (n) *soopermarket*
supplement επιβάρυνση (f) *epeevareensee*
surfboard σερφ (n) *serf*
surfing/wind surfing σέρφινγκ (n) *serfeeng*
sweater πουλόβερ (n) *poolover*
sweet/cake γλυκό (n) *ghleeko*
sweets καραμέλες (f) *karameles*
swimming costume μαγιό (n) *mayo*
swimming pool πισίνα (f) *peeseena*
to switch on ανάβω *anavo*
syrup σιρόπι (n) *seeropee*

T

table τραπέζι (n) *trapezee*
to take παίρνω (θα πάρω) *perno (tha paro)*
taken (seat) πιασμένος, -η, -ο *peeazmenos-ee-o*
to take off (clothes) βγάζω *vghazo*
tampons ταμπόν *tabon*
tangerine μανταρίνι (n) *mandareenee*
tap βρύση (f) *vreesee*
tax φόρος (m) *foros*
taxi ταξί (n) *taksee*
taxi rank πιάτσα ταξί (f) *peeatsa taksee*
tea τσάι (n) *tsaee*
teaspoon κουταλάκι (n) *kootalakee*
telephone τηλέφωνο (n) *teelefono*
telephone card τηλεκάρτα (f) *teelekarta*
television τηλεόραση (f) *teeleorasee*
temporary προσωρινός *prosoreenos*
tennis court γήπεδο τένις (n) *yeepedo tenees*
tent σκηνή (f) *skeenee*
terrace βεράντα (f) *veranda*
thank you ευχαριστώ *efhareesto*
that εκείνος, -η, -ο *ekeenos-ee-o*
the ο (m) η (f) το (n) *o ee to*
theatre θέατρο (n) *theatro*
then/after μετά *meta*
there is/are υπάρχει/υπάρχουν *eeparhee/eeparhoon*
there it is νάτος, -η, -ο *natos-ee-o*
these αυτά *afta*
to think νομίζω/σκέφτομαι *nomeezo/skeftome*
this αυτός, -η, -ο *aftos-ee-o*
ticket εισιτήριο (n) *eeseeteereeo*
adult tickets κανονικά εισιτήρια *kanoneeka eeseeteereea*
ticket office εκδοτήριο (n) *ekdhoteereeo*
till ταμείο (n) *tameeo*
time φορά/ώρα *fora/ora*
timetable δρομολόγιο (n) *dhromoloyeeo*
tin κονσέρβα (f) *konserva*
tip φιλοδώρημα (n) *feelodhoreema*
tissues χαρτομάντιλα (n) *hartomandeela*
to (distance) να *na*
to (time) παρά *para*
to, on, at σε, σ' *se, s'*
toast φρυγανιά (f) *freeganeea*
today σήμερα *seemera*
toilets τουαλέτες (f) *tooaletes*
tomato ντομάτα (f) *domata*
tomorrow αύριο *avreeo*
tooth δόντι (n) *dhondee*
toothache πονόδοντος (m) *ponodhondos*

toothbrush οδοντόβουρτσα (f) *odhondovoortsa*
toothpaste οδοντόκρεμα (f) *odhondokrema*
tour ξενάγηση (f) *ksenayeesee*
towel πετσέτα (f) *petseta*
town walls τείχη της πόλης (n) *teehee tees polees*
train τρένο (n) *treno*
travel agency ταξιδιωτικό πρακτορείο (n) *takseedheeoteeko praktoreeo*
traveller's cheques ταξιδιωτική επιταγή (f) *takseedheeoteekee epeetayee*
triple (room) τρίκλινο (n) *treekleeno*
trousers παντελόνι (n) *pandelonee*
to try δοκιμάζω *dhokeemazo*
T-shirt φανελάκι (n) *fanelakee*
to turn στρίβω *streevo*
tyre λάστιχο (n) *lasteeho*

U

(beach) umbrella ομπρέλα (f) *ombrela*
to understand καταλαβαίνω *katalaveno*
underwear εσώρουχα (n) *esorooha*
unfortunately δυστυχώς *dheesteehos*
unleaded αμόλυβδη (f) *amoleevdee*
urgent επείγον *epeeghon*
to use χρησιμοποιώ *hreeseemopeeo*

V

to validate επικυρώνω *epeekeerono*
vase βάζο (n) *vazo*
vegetarian χορτοφάγος *hortofaghos*
vegetarian dishes λαδερά (n) *ladhera*
very well πολύ καλά *polee kala*
very/a lot πολύ *polee*
villa βίλα (f) *veela*
vinegar ξίδι (n) *kseedhee*

W

to wake up ξυπνάω *kseepnao*
wallet/purse πορτοφόλι (n) *portofolee*
to want θέλω *thelo*
I'd like θα ήθελα *tha eethela*
washbasin νιπτήρας (m) *neepteeras*
washing powder απορρυπαντικό (n) *aporeepandeeko*
water νερό (n) *nero*
watermelon καρπούζι (n) *karpoozee*
waterskis σκι (n) *skee*
weather καιρός (m) *keros*
week εβδομάδα (f) *evdhomadha*
what τι *tee*
wheel ρόδα (f) *rodha*
when? πότε; *pote*
where? πού; *poo*
which/which one? ποιος,-α, -ο; *peeos-a-o*
white άσπρος, -η, -ο *aspros-ee-o*
window παράθυρο (n) *paratheero*
windscreen wiper υαλοκαθαριστήρας (m) *eealokathareesteeras*
wine κρασί (n) *krasee*
with, from, till, by με *me*
without χωρίς *horees*
woollen μάλλινο *maleeno*
to work (function) λειτουργώ *leetoorgho*
worry beads κομπολόι (n) *koboloee*

Y

yellow κίτρινος, -η, -ο *keetreenos-ee-o*
yes ναι *ne*
yes, of course βεβαίως *veveos*
yesterday χθες *hthes*
yoghurt γιαούρτι (n) *yaoortee*
your (pl) σας *sas*
youth hostel ξενώνας νεότητας (m) *ksenonas neoteetas*

α

αγγούρι (n) cucumber *angooree*
αγκώνας (m) elbow *angonas*
αγορά (f) market *aghora*
αγοράζω to buy *aghorazo*
αέρας (m) air *aeras*
αεροδρόμιο (n) airport *aerodhromeeo*
αεροπλάνο (n) aeroplane *aeroplano*
αίθουσα (f) room *ethoosa*
ακόμα still, even *akoma*
αλάβαστρο (n) alabaster *alavastro*
αλάτι (n) salt *alatee*
αλεύρι (n) flour *alevree*
αλλάζω to change *alazo*
αλλεργικό συνάχι (n) hayfever *aleryeeko seenahee*
αλλεργικός, -η, -ο allergic *aleryeekos*
άλλος, -η, -ο other *alos-ee-o*
αλοιφή (f) lotion *aleefee*
αμόλυβδη (f) unleaded *amoleevdee*
ανάβω to switch on *anavo*
αναπνευστήρας (m) snorkel *anapnefsteeras*
αναπνέω to breathe *anapneo*
αναχώρηση (f) departure *anahoreesee*
αναψυκτικό (n) soft drink *anapseekteeko*
Ανδρών (m) Gents *andhron*
ανθρακούχο, με ανθρακικό sparkling *anthrakooho, me anthrakeeko*
ανοιχτός, -η, -ο open *aneehtos-ee-o*
αντιβιοτικό (n) antibiotics *andeeveeoteeko*
αντιισταμινικό (n) antihistamine *andee-eestameeneeko*
απλό εισιτήριο one way *aplo eeseeteereeo*
από from *apo*
αποβάθρα (f) platform *apovathra*
απόδειξη (f) receipt *apodheeksee*
αποδυτήρια (n) changing rooms *apodheeteereea*
απορρυπαντικό (n) washing powder *aporeepandeeko*
αποσμητικό (n) deodorant *apozmeeteeko*
αρακάς (m) peas *arakas*
αρέσω to like *areso*
μου αρέσει I like *moo aresee*
αριθμός (m) number *areethmos*
αριθμός κυκλοφορίας car registration number *areethmos keekloforeeas*
αριστερά left *areestera*
αρκετά enough *arketa*
άρρωστος, -η, -ο ill *arostos-ee-o*
αρχαιότητες (f, pl) antiquities *arheoteetes*
αρχίζω to begin *arheezo*
ασανσέρ (n) lift *asanser*
ασημικά (n) silverware *aseemeeka*
ασθενοφόρο (n) ambulance *asthenoforo*
ασπιρίνη (f) aspirin *aspeereenee*
άσπρος, -η, -ο white *aspros*
αστράγαλος (o) ankle *astraghalos*
αστυνομία (f) police *asteenomeea*
αστυνομικό τμήμα (n) police station *asteenomeeko tmeema*
ασφάλεια (f) insurance *asfaleea*
άτομο (n) person *atomo*
αυγό (n) egg *avgho*
αύριο tomorrow *avreeo*
αυτά these *afta*
αυτί (n) ear *aftee*
αυτοκίνητο (n) car *aftokeeneeto*
αυτός, -η, -ο this *aftos-ee-o*
αφήνω to leave *afeeno*
άφιξη (f) arrival *afeeksee*
αχλάδι (n) pear *ahladee*
άψητος, -η, -ο raw *apseetos-ee-o*

β

βάζο (n) vase/jar *vazo*
βάζω to put *vazo*
βαλίτσα (f) suitcase *valeetsa*
βαμβακερό cotton (fabric) *vamvakero*
βατραχοπέδιλα (npl) flippers *vatrahopedheela*
βγάζω to take off *vghazo*
βεβαίως yes, of course *veveos*
βεράντα (f) terrace *veranda*
βερίκοκο (n) apricot *vereekoko*
βεστιάριο (n) cloakroom *vesteeareeo*
βιβλίο (n) book *veevleeo*
βιβλιοπωλείο (n) bookshop *veevleeopoleeo*
βίλα (f) villa *veela*
βλέπω to see *vlepo*
βοήθεια help *voeetheea*
βοηθώ to help *voeetho*
βορράς (m) North *voras*

βράδυ (n), βραδιά evening *vradhee/vradheea*
βρεφική τροφή (f) baby food *vrefeekee trofee*
βρύση (f) tap *vreesee*

γ

γάλα (n) milk *ghala*
γαλακτοπωλείο (n) dairy shop *ghalaktopoleeo*
γαλάκτωμα για μετά τον ήλιο (n) after-sun lotion *ghalaktoma ya meta ton eeleeo*
γεια σας hello/goodbye (pl) *ya sas*
γεια σου hello/goodbye (sing) *ya soo*
γεμάτος, -η, -ο full *yematos-ee-o*
γεμίζω to fill up *gemeezo*
γεμιστά (n) stuffed *yemeesta*
γέφυρα (f) bridge *yefeera*
γήπεδο (n) stadium *yeepedo*
γήπεδο τένις (n) tennis court *yeepedo tenees*
για for *ya*
γιαούρτι (n) yoghurt *yaoortee*
γιατρός (m) doctor *yatros*
γιος (m) son *yos*
γκρέιπ φρουτ (n) grapefruit *greeep froot*
γκρίζος, -α, -ο grey *ghreezos-a-o*
γλυκό (n) sweet/cake *ghleeko*
γόνατο (n) knee *ghonato*
γοφός (m) hip *ghofos*
γράμμα (n) letter *ghrama*
γραμμάριο (n) gramme *ghramareeo*
γραμματόσημο (n) stamp *ghramatoseemo*
γυαλιά ηλίου (n) sunglasses *yaleea eeleeoo*
γυαλιστερές (φωτογραφίες) glossy (photo prints) *yaleesteres (fotoghrafeees)*
γυμναστήριο (n) fitness centre *yeemnasteereeo*
γυναικών (f) Ladies (toilets) *yeenekon*
γρανίτα (f) sherbet (crushed ice drink) *ghraneeta*

δ

δαγκώνω to bite *dhangono*
δάχτυλο (n) finger *dhahteelo*
δείχνω to show *deehno*
δεν not *dhen*
δεξιά on the right *dhekseea*
δερμάτινο leather (item) *dhermateeno*
δεύτερος, -η, -ο second *defteros*
διαβατήριο (n) passport *dheeavateereeo*
διαβητικός, -η, -ο diabetic *dheeaveeteekos-ee-o*
διάλειμμα (n) interval *dheealeema*
διαμέρισμα (n) apartment *dheeamereesma*
διάρροια (f) diarrhoea *deeareea*
διασκέδαση (f) entertainment *dheeaskedasee*
διεύθυνση (f) address *dheeeftheensee*
δίκλινο double (room) *dheekleeno*
δίνω to give *dheeno*
διπλός, -η, -ο double (food portion, drinks measure) *dheeplos-ee-o*
δίπλωμα (n) driving license *dheeploma*
δοκιμάζω to try *dhokeemazo*
δόντι (n) tooth *dhondee*
δρομολόγιο (n) timetable *dhromoloyeeo*
δρόμος (m) street *dhromos*
δυσκοιλιότητα (f) constipation *dheeskeeleeoteeta*
δυστυχώς unfortunately *dheesteehos*
δωμάτιο (n) room *dhomateeo*

ε

εβδομάδα (f) week *evdhomadha*
εγχείρηση (f) operation *enheereesee*
εδώ here *edho*
είμαι to be *eeme*
εισιτήριο (n) ticket *eeseeteereeo*
εκδοτήριο (n) ticket office *ekdhoteereeo*
εκείνος, -η, -ο that *ekeenos-ee-o*
εκκλησία (f) church *ekleeseea*
έκπτωση (f) concession *ekptosee*
ελέγχω (ελέγξτε) check *elenho (elenkste)*
ελεύθερος, -η, -ο free *eleftheros-ee-o*

Ελληνικά (n) Greek (language) *eleeneeka*
εμπορικό κέντρο shopping centre *emboreeko kendro*
εμφανίζω to develop *emfaneezo*
εμφιαλωμένος, -η, -ο bottled (water) *emfeealomenos-ee-o*
ένας/ένα (m, n) a, an/one *enas/ena*
ενδιαφέρω interest *endheeafero*
εντάξει OK *endaksee*
έντομο (n) insect *endomo*
έντυπο (n) form *endeepo*
έξοδος exit *eksodhos*
εξωτερική γραμμή outside line (telephone call) *eksotereekee ghramee*
εξωτερικός, -η, -ο outer *eksotereekos*
επαναλαμβάνω to repeat *epanalamvano*
επείγον urgent *epeeghon*
επιβάρυνση (f) supplement *epeevareensee*
επιδόρπιο (n) dessert *epeedhorpeeo*
επικυρώνω to validate *epeekeerono*
επιστροφή (f) return *epeestrofee*
επόμενο next *epomeno*
ερ κοντίσιον (n) air conditioning *er kondeeseeon*
έργο (θεατρικό) (n) play (theatre) *ergho (theatreeko)*
εστιατόριο (n) restaurant *esteeatoreeo*
εσώρουχα (npl) underwear *esorooha*
εσωτερικός, -η, -ο inner *esotereekos-ee-o*
έτοιμος ready *eteemos*
ευθεία (f) straight on *eftheea*
ευρώ (n) euro *evro*
ευχαριστώ thank you *efhareesto*
έχω (έχετε ...) to have (do you have?) *eho (ehete)*

ζ

ζακέτα (f) jacket (women's) *zaketa*
ζαμπόν (n) ham *zambon*
ζάχαρη (f) sugar *zaharee*
ζαχαροπλαστείο (n) patisserie *zaharoplasteeo*
ζεστός hot *zestos-ee-o*
ζυγός, -η, -ο even *zeeghos-ee-o*
ζυμαρικά (n, pl) pasta *zeemareeka*
ζώνη (f) belt *zonee*

η

η the (f) *ee*
ή or *ee*
ήλιος (m) sun *eeleeos*
ημέρα (f) day *eemera*
ημερήσια εκδρομή (f) day trip *eemereeseea ekdhromee*
ημιδιατροφή (f) half board *eemeedeeatrofee*
ήσυχος, -η, -ο alone *eeseehos*
άσε με ήσυχο leave me alone *ase me eeseeho*

θ

θα shall/will *tha*
θέατρο (n) theatre *theatro*
θέλω to want *thelo*
θα ήθελα I'd like *tha eethela*
θέση (f) class *thesee*
θυρίδα (f) safety box *theereedha*

ι

ίδιος, -α, -ο same *eedheeos*
ιντερνέτ (n) internet *eenternet*
ιππόδρομος (m) race course *eepodhromos*
Ιπτάμενο Δελφίνι (n) Flying Dolphin *eeptameno dhelfeenee*
ίσια straight *eeseea*
ισόγειο (n) ground floor *eesoyeeo*
ιστιοπλοΐα (f) sailing *eesteeoploeea*
ιχθυοπωλείο fishmonger's *eehtheeopoleeo*

κ

και and *ke*
καΐκι (n) sailing boat/dinghy *kaeekee*
καιρός (m) weather *keros*
καίω to burn *keo*
Καλή όρεξη! (f) Enjoy your meal! *kalee oreksee*
καλημέρα good morning *kaleemera*
καληνύχτα good night *kaleeneehta*
καλησπέρα good evening *kaleespera*
καλοριφέρ (n) central heating *kaloreefer*
καλός, -ή, -ο good *kalos-ee-o*
κάλτσες (f) socks *kaltses*
καλώ to call *kalo*
κάμπινγκ (n) campsite *kampeeng*
καμπίνα (f) cabin *kabeena*

κανένας someone *kanenas*
κανονικά (εισιτήρια) standard (adult tickets) *kanoneeka (eeseeteereea)*
κάνω to do *kano*
καπέλο (n) hat *kapelo*
καπνίζω to smoke *kapneezo*
κάποιος, -α, -ο someone *kapeeos-a-o*
κάπου somewhere *kapoo*
καράβι (n) ship *karavee*
καραμέλες (f) sweets *karameles*
καρδιά (f) heart *kardheea*
καρότα (n) carrots *karota*
καρπούζι (n) watermelon *karpoozee*
κάρτα (f) postcard *karta*
κάρτα μνήμης (f) memory card *karta mneemees*
κάρτες (f) postcards *kartes*
κάστρο (n) castle *kastro*
καταλαβαίνω to understand *katalaveno*
κατάλογος (m) menu *kataloghos*
κατάστημα (ενδυμάτων) (n) (clothes) shop *katasteema (endheematon)*
κάτι something/anything *katee*
καφέ brown *kafe*
καφές (m) coffee *kafes*
κεντρικός, -η, -ο central/main *kendreekos-ee-o*
κέντρο (n) centre *kendro*
κεραμικά (n) ceramics *kerameeka*
κεράσι (n) cherry *kerasee*
κεφάλι (n) head *kefalee*
κήπος (m) garden *keepos*
κιλό (n) kilo *keelo*
κιμάς (μοσχαρίσιος) minced (beef) *keemas (mos-hareeseeos)*
κινούμαι to move *keenoome*
κίτρινος, -η, -ο yellow *keetreenos-ee-o*
κλαμπ (n) nightclub *klab*
κλειδαριά (f) lock *kleedhareea*
κλειδί (n) key *kleedhee*
κλείνω to close/hang up/switch off/reserve *kleeno*
κόβω to cut *kovo*
κόκαλο (n) bone *kokalo*
κόκκινος, -η, -ο red *kokkeenos-ee-o*
κολιέ (n) necklace *koleee*
κολοκυθάκι (n) courgette *kolokeethakee*
κολόνια (f) eau de cologne *koloneea*
κομμωτήριο (n) hairdresser's *komoteereeo*
κομπολόι (n) worry beads *koboloee*
κονσέρβα (f) tin *konserva*
κοντά near *konda*
κοντινός, -η, -ο close *kondeenos-ee-o*
κόρη (f) daughter *koree*
κόσμημα (n) jewellery *kozmeema*
κοστίζω to cost *kosteezo*
κοτόπουλο (n) chicken *kotopoolo*
κουβέρτα (f) blanket *kooverta*
κουκέτα (f) couchette *kooketa*
κουλουράκι (n) cookie *kooloorakee*
κουταλάκι (n) teaspoon *kootolakee*
κουτάλι (n) spoon *kootalee*
κρασί (n) wine *krasee*
κρατάω to keep *kratao*
κρεατικό (n) meat dish *kreateeko*
κρεβάτι (n) bed, sun lounger *krevatee*
κρέμα (f) cream *krema*
  κρέμα χεριών (f) hand cream *krema hereeon*
κρεμμύδι (n) onion *kremeedhee*
κρεοπωλείο (n) butcher *kreopoleeo*
κρέπα (f) pancake *krepa*
κρύος, -α, -ο cold *kreeos-a-o*
κύριος main *keereeos*

λ

λαδερά (n) vegetarian dishes *ladhera*
λάδι (n) oil *ladhee*
λάθος (n) mistake *lathos*
λαιμός (m) neck *lemos*
λάμπα (f) lamp *lamba*
λαμπατέρ (n) lamp (standard) *labater*
λαστιχένια βάρκα (f) rubber dinghy *lasteeheneea varka*
λάστιχο (n) tyre *lasteeho*
λάχανο (n) cabbage *lahano*
λέγομαι my name is *leghome*
λειτουργώ to work (function) *leetoorgho*
  λειτουργεί it works *leetooryee*
λεμονάδα (f) lemonade *lemonadha*

λεμόνι (n) lemon *lemonee*
λεπτά (euro) cents *lepta*
λεπτό (n) minute *lepto*
λεφτά (n) money *lefta*
λεωφορείο (n) bus *leoforeeo*
λίγο a bit *leegho*
λίγος, -η, -ο little/a little *leeghos-ee-o*
λιγότερο, πιο λίγο less *leeghotero, peeo leegho*
λιμάνι (n) port *leemanee*
λίρα (f) pound *leera*
λίτρο (n) litre *leetro*
λογαριασμός (m) bill *logareeasmos*

μ

μαγαζί (n) shop *maghazee*
μαγιό (n) swimming costume *mayo*
μάθημα (n) lesson *matheema*
μακριά far *makreea*
μάλιστα certainly/of course *maleesta*
μάλλινο woollen *maleeno*
μανάβικο (n) greengrocer's *manaveeko*
μανιτάρια (n) mushrooms *maneetareea*
μανταρίνι (n) tangerine *mandareenee*
μαντήλι (n) scarf, handkerchief *mandeelee*
μαξιλάρι (n) pillow *makseelaree*
μαρμελάδα (f) jam *marmeladha*
μαρούλι (n) lettuce *maroolee*
μάσκα θαλάσσης (f) swimming mask *maska thalasees*
ματ matt *mat*
μάτι (n) eye *matee*
μαύρος, -η, -ο black *mavros-ee-o*
μαχαίρι (n) knife *maheree*
με with, from, till, by *me*
μεγάλος, -η, -ο adult, big *meghalos-ee-o*
μέλι (n) honey *melee*
μελιτζάνα (f) aubergine *meleedsana*
μενού (n) menu of the day *menoo*
μένω to stay *meno*
μέρα (f) day *mera*
μεσάνυχτα midnight *mesaneehta*
μεσημέρι (n) midday *meseemeree*
μετά then/after *meta*
μεταξωτό silk *metaksoto*
μετασχηματιστής (m) travel adaptor *metas-heemateestees*
μετρητά (n) cash *metreeta*
μέτριος, -α, -ο medium *metreeos-a-o*
μέτρο (n) meter *metro*
μέχρι as far as/until *mehree*
μήλο (n) apple *meelo*
μητρόπολη (f) cathedral *meetropolee*
μία (f) a, an/one (fem) *meea*
μιας χρήσεως single use *meeas hreeseos*
μικρός, -η, -ο small *meekros-ee-o*
μικρότερος, -η, -ο smaller *meekroteros-ee-o*
μιλάω to speak *meelao*
μισός half *meesos*
μισοτιμής half price *meesoteemees*
μνήμη (f) memory *mneemee*
μόνο only *monos-ee-o*
μονόκλινο (n) single room *monokleeno*
μονός, -η, -ο odd *monos*
μου mine/to me *moo*
μου δίνετε I'd like *moo dheenete*
μουσείο (n) museum *mooseeo*
μπάλα (f) ball *bala*
μπαλκόνι (n) veranda *balkonee*
μπάμιες (fpl) okra *bamee-es*
μπανάνα (f) banana *banana*
μπάνιο (n) bathroom *baneeo*
μπαρ (n) bar *bar*
μπάσκετ (n) basketball *basket*
μπαστούνι του γκολφ (n) golf club *bastoonee too golf*
μπαταρία (f) battery *batareea*
μπεζ beige *bez*
μπισκότο (n) biscuit *beeskoto*
μπλε blue *ble*
μπολ (n) bowl *bol*
μπορώ can (to be able) *boro*
μπότα (f) boot *bota*
μπουκάλι (n) bottle *bookalee*
μπρατσάκια (npl) armbands *bratsakeea*
μπριζόλα (f) chop (of meat) *breezola*
μπρούτζινα (n, pl) brass objects *broodseena*
μπύρα (f) beer *beera*
μύτη (f) nose *meetee*

ν

να to *na*
ναι yes *ne*
νάτος, -η, -ο there it is *natos-ee-o*
νερό (n) water *nero*
νεφρό (n) kidney *nefro*
νησιά (npl) islands *neeseea*
νιπτήρας (m) washbasin *neepteeras*
νοικιάζω to rent *neekeeazo*
νομίζω to think *nomeezo*
νοσοκομείο (n) hospital *nosokomeeo*
νοσοκόμος (m)/νοσοκόμα (f) nurse *nosokomos/nosokoma*
νοστιμότατος delicious *nosteemotatos*
Νότος (m) South *notos*
νούμερο (n) size/number *noomero*
ντομάτα (f) tomato *domata*
ντόπιος local *dopeeos*
ντους (n) shower *doos*

ξ

ξαπλώστρα (f) deckchair *ksaplostra*
ξενάγηση (f) tour *ksenayeesee*
ξεναγός (m, f) guide *ksenagos*
ξενοδοχείο (n) hotel *ksenodhoheeo*
ξενώνας νεότητας (m) Youth Hostel *ksenonas neoteetas*
ξέρω to know *ksero*
ξίδι (n) vinegar *kseedhee*
ξυπνάω to wake up *kseepnao*

ο

ο, η, το the *o, ee, to*
οδηγός (m) guide (book) *odheeghos*
οδοντίατρος (m/f) dentist *odhondeeatros*
οδοντόβουρτσα (f) toothbrush *odhondovoortsa*
οδοντόκρεμα (f) toothpaste *odhondokrema*
οδός (f) street *odhos*
όλα μαζί altogether *ola mazee*
ομπρέλα (f) (beach) umbrella *ombrela*
όνομα (n) name *onoma*
ορειβασία (f) climbing *oreevaseea*
ορίστε here (you are/it is)/pardon *oreeste*
όροφος (m) floor *orofos*
όχι no *ohee*

π

πάγος (m) ice *paghos*
παγωτό (n) ice cream *paghoto*
παιδί (n) child *pedhee*
παιδικός, -η, -ο for children *pedheekos-ee-o*
παίζω to play *pezo*
παίρνω (θα πάρω ...) to take (it will take ...) *perno (tha paro)*
πακέτο (n) pocket *paketo*
παλτό (n) overcoat *palto*
πάνες (f) nappies *panes*
πανσιόν (f) guesthouse *panseeon*
παντελόνι (n) trousers *pandelonee*
παντζούρι (n) shutter *padsooree*
παντοπωλείο (n) grocery shop *pandopoleeo*
παπούτσι (n) shoe *papootsee*
παρά to (time) *para*
παραγγέλνω to order *parangelno*
παράθυρο (n) window *paratheero*
παρακαλώ please *parakalo*
παρακαλώ you're welcome/don't mention it *parakalo*
παραλία (f) beach *paraleea*
παρκάρω to park *parkaro*
πάρκινγκ (n) car park *parkeeng*
πάρκο (n) park *parko*
πάστα (f) pastry *pasta*
πατάτα (f) potato *patata*
πάω to go *pao*
πέδιλα (n) sandals *pedheela*
πεζόδρομος (m) pedestrian zone *pezodhromos*
πειράζει it matters *peerazee*
πεπόνι (n) melon *peponee*
περιέχει it contains *pereeehee*
περιλαμβάνομαι to be included *pereelamvanome*
περιοδικό (n) magazine *pereeodheeko*
περίπτερο (n) kiosk *pereeptero*
περνάω to pass (on road) *pernao*
πετρέλαιο (n) oil *petreleo*
πετσέτα (f) towel *petseta*
πετσέτα (f) napkin *petseta*
πιασμένος, -η, -ο taken (seat) *peeazmenos-ee-o*

πιατάκι (n) saucer *peeatakee*
πιάτο (n) plate/course *peeato*
πιάτσα ταξί (f) taxi rank *peeatsa taksee*
πινακοθήκη (f) gallery *peenakotheekee*
πίνω to drink *peeno*
πιο αργά more slowly *peeo arga*
πιο κάτω further on *peeo kato*
πιπέρι (n) pepper (spice) *peeperee*
πιπεριά (f) pepper (vegetable) *peepereea*
πιρούνι (n) fork *peeroonee*
πισίνα (f) swimming pool *peeseena*
πιστολάκι (n) hairdryer *peestolakee*
πιστωτική κάρτα (f) credit card *peestoteekee karta*
πλατεία (f) square *plateea*
πλάτη (f) back *platee*
πλατφόρμα (f) platform *platforma*
πληροφορία (f) information *pleeroforeea*
πληρώνω to pay *pleerono*
πλυντήριο (n) laundry *pleendeereeo*
ποδήλατο (n) bike *podheelato*
πόδι (n) foot *podhee*
ποδόσφαιρο (n) football *podhosfero*
ποιος; which/which one? *peeos*
πολύ very/a lot *polee*
πολύ καλά very well *polee kala*
πολυκατάστημα (n) department store *poleekatasteema*
πονάω to ache/hurt *ponao*
πονόδοντος (m) toothache *ponodhondos*
πονοκέφαλος (m) headache *ponokefalos*
πόρτα (f) door *porta*
πορτοκαλάδα (f) orangeade *portokaladha*
πορτοκάλι (n) orange *portokalee*
πορτοφόλι (n) wallet/purse *portofolee*
πόσο; how much? *poso*
πόσο έχει; how much is it? *poso ehee*
πόσο κάνει; how much is it? *poso kanee*
πότε; when? *pote*
ποτήρι (n) glass *poteeree*
ποτό (n) drink *poto*
πού; where? *poo*
πουκάμισο (n) shirt *pookameeso*
πουλόβερ (n) sweater *poolover*
πράσινος, -η, -ο green *praseenos*
πρέπει to have to *prepee*
πρόβλημα (n) problem *provleema*
πρόγραμμα (n) programme *proghrama*
προσωρινός temporary *prosoreenos*
προτεραιότητα (f) priority *protereoteeta*
προφυλακτικό (n) condom *profeelakteeko*
πρόχειρο φαγητό (n) snacks *proheero fayeeto*
πρωί (n) morning *proee*
πρωινό (n) breakfast *proeeno*
πρώτος, -η, -ο first *protos*
πτήση (f) flight *pteesee*
πυρετός (m) fever *peeretos*
πυροτεχνήματα (n) fireworks *peerotehneemata*
πώς? how? *pos*
πώς λέγεστε; what's your name? *pos leyeste*
πώς σου φαίνεται;/πώς σας φαίνεται; how do you like it? *pos soo fenete/pos sas fenete*

ρ

ρακέτα (f) racket *raketa*
ρέστα (n) change (coins) *resta*
ρίγανη (f) oregano *reeghanee*
ρόδα (f) wheel *rodha*
ροδάκινο (n) peach *rodhakeeno*
ροζ pink *roz*
ρόκα (f) rocket *roka*
ρολό (n) blind *rolo*
ρουμ σέρβις (n) room service *room servees*
ρούχα (n) clothes *rooha*

σ

σαγιονάρες (fpl) flip flops *sayeeonares*
σακάκι (n) jacket *sakakee*
σακουλάκι (n) sachet *sakoolakee*
σαλάτα (f) salad *salata*
σαμπουάν (n) shampoo *sampooan*
σάντουιτς (n) sandwich *sandooeets*
σάουνα (f) sauna *saoona*
σαπούνι (n) soap *sapoonee*

σας your (pl) *sas*
σε, σ' to, on, at *se, s'*
σελφ σέρβις (n) self-service *self servees*
σεντόνι (n) sheet *sendonee*
σερβιέτες (fpl) sanitary towels *serveeetes*
σερφ (n) surfboard *serf*
σέρφινγκ (n) surfing/wind surfing *serfeeng*
σεσουάρ (n) hairdryer *sesooar*
σήμερα today *seemera*
σίδερο (n) iron *seedhero*
σινεμά (n) cinema *seenema*
σιρόπι (n) syrup *seeropee*
σιρόπι για το βήχα cough mixture *seeropee ya to veeha*
σκάλα (f) stairs *skala*
σκάφος (n) boat *skafos*
σκέφτομαι to think *skeftome*
σκηνή (f) tent *skeenee*
σκι (n) skiing/waterskiing *skee*
σκόρδο (n) garlic *skordho*
σκουπιδοντενεκές (m) dustbin *skoopeedhondenekes*
σκούρος, -η, -ο dark *skooros-ee-o*
σκύλος (m) dog *skeelos*
σοβαρός, -η, -ο serious *sovaros-ee-o*
σοκολάτα (f) chocolate *sokolata*
σορτς (n) shorts *sorts*
σούπερ μάρκετ (n) supermarket *soopermarket*
σπανάκι (n) spinach *spanakee*
σπάω to break *spao*
σπεσιαλιτέ (f) speciality *speseealeete*
σπίρτα (n) matches *speerta*
στάδιο stadium *stadheeo*
στάθμευση (f) parking *stathmefsee*
σταθμός (m) station (bus, rail) *stathmos*
στάση (f) bus stop *stasee*
σταφύλια (npl) grapes *stafeeleea*
στέλνω to send *stelno*
στήθος (n) chest *steethos*
στις (fpl) in, on, at, to *stees*
στοματικό διάλυμα (n) mouthwash *stomateeko dheealeema*
στομάχι (n) stomach *stomahee*
στον (m), στην (f), στο (n) at, to, on, in the *ston, steen, sto*
στρίβω to turn *streevo*
στυλό (n) pen *steelo*
συγνώμη (f) excuse me/I'm sorry/ pardon *seeghnomee*
σύκο (n) fig *seeko*
συκώτι (n) liver *seekotee*
συμπληρώνω to fill in *seembleerono*
συναυλία (f) concert *seenavleea*
συνδέω, συνδέομαι to connect *seendheo, seendheome*
συνταγή (f) prescription *seendayee*
συνταξιούχος (m/f) pensioner *seendakseeoohos*
συστήνω to recommend *seesteeno*
σφράγισμα (n) filling (tooth) *sfrayeesma*
σχέδιο (n) plan *sh-edheeo*
σωσίβιο (n) life belt *soseeveeo*

T

τάβλι (n) backgammon *tavlee*
ταμείο (n) till *tameeo*
ταξί (n) taxi *taksee*
ταξιδιωτική επιταγή (f) traveller's cheques *takseedheeoteekee epeetayee*
ταξιδιωτικό πρακτορείο (n) travel agency *takseedheeoteeko praktoreeo*
τείχη της πόλης (n) town walls *teehee tees polees*
τελειώνω (τελείωσε) to finish (we've run out) *teleeono (teleeose)*
τέλος (n) end *telos*
τεχνητές ίνες (f) man-made fibres *tehneetes eenes*
τζαμί (n) mosque *tzamee*
τζιν (n) jeans *dseen*
τηλεκάρτα (f) telephone card *teelekarta*
τηλεόραση (f) television *teeleorasee*
τηλέφωνο (n) telephone *teelefono*
τι; what? *tee*
τι κάνεις;/τι κάνετε; how are you? *tee kanees/tee kanete*
τιμόνι (n) steering wheel *teemonee*
τίποτ' άλλο anything else *teepot alo*
τμήμα (n) department *tmeema*

τουαλέτες (f) toilets *tooaletes*
τραγούδι (n) song *traghoodhee*
τράπεζα bank *trapeza*
τραπέζι (n) table *trapezee*
τρένο (n) train *treno*
τρίκλινο (n) triple (room) *treekleeno*
τροχόσπιτο (n) caravan *trohospeeto*
τσάι (n) tea *tsaee*
τσάντα (f) bag *tsanda*
τσιγάρα (n) cigarettes *tseeghara*
τσιμπάω to sting *tseembao*
τσίμπημα (n) sting *tseembeema*
τσίχλα (f) chewing gum *tseehla*
τσουρέκι (n) type of brioche *tsoorekee*
τυρί (n) cheese *teeree*

υ

υαλοκαθαριστήρας (m) windscreen wiper *eealokathareesteeras*
υγρό φακών επαφής (n) contact lens solution *eeghro fakon epafees*
υπάρχει/υπάρχουν there is/are *eeparhee/eeparhoon*
υπόγειο (n) basement *eepoyeeo*
υπογράφω to sign *eepoghrafo*
υπότιτλος (m) subtitle *eepoteetlos*

φ

φακοί επαφής (m) contact lenses *fakee epafees*
φανάρι (n) light *fanaree*
φανελάκι (n) T-shirt *fanelakee*
φαρμακείο (n) chemist's *farmakeeo*
φάρμακο (n) medicine *farmako*
φασολάκια (n) green beans *fasolakeea*
φέρνω to bring *ferno*
φέρυ μπόουτ (n) ferry *feree booot*
φεστιβάλ (n) festival *festeeval*
φέτα (f) slice/type of cheese *feta*
φεύγω to leave *fevgho*
φθηνότερο cheaper *ftheenotero*
φιλμ (n) film *feelm*
φιλοδώρημα (n) tip *feelodhoreema*
φλυτζάνι (n) cup *fleedsanee*
φοιτητές (m) students *feeteetees*
φόρεμα (n) dress *forema*
φόρος (m) tax *foros*
φούρνος (m) bakery *foornos*
φούστα (f) shirt *foosta*
φράουλα (f) strawberry *fraoola*
φρούτο (n) fruit *frooto*
φρυγανιά (f) toast *freeghaneea*
φτάνω to arrive *ftano*
φύλαξη αποσκευών left luggage *feelaksee aposkevon*
φωνάζω to shout *fonazo*
φως (n) light *fos*
φωτογραφία (f) photograph *fotoghrafeea*
φωτογραφική μηχανή (f) camera *fotoghrafeekee meehanee*

χ

χαίρω πολύ pleased to meet you *hero polee*
παθαίνω βλάβη to break down *patheno vlavee*
χαλί (n) carpet *halee*
χανζαπλάστ (n) plasters *hanzaplast*
χάνω to lose *hano*
χάπι (n) pill *hapee*
χάρτης (m) map *hartees*
χαρτί (n) paper *hartee*
χαρτομάντιλα (n) tissues *hartomandeela*
χαρτοφύλακας (m) briefcase *hartofeelakas*
χέρι (n) hand *heree*
χθες yesterday *hthes*
χορτοφάγος vegetarian *hortofaghos*
χρειάζομαι to need *hreeazome*
χρησιμοποιώ to use *hreeseemopeeo*
χρώμα (n) colour *hroma*
χυμός (m) juice *heemos*
χωρίς without *horees*

ψ

ψαράδικο (n) fishmonger's *psaradheeko*
ψάρι (n) fish *psaree*
ψήνω to cook *pseeno*
ψηφιακή μηχανή (f) digital camera *pseefeeakee meehanee*
ψυγείο (n) fridge *pseeyeeo*
ψωμί (n) bread *psomee*

ω

ώμος (m) shoulder *omos*
ώρα hour/time *ora*
ωραίος, -α, -ο nice *oreos-a-o*